WHAT OTHERS ARE SAYING ABOUT GREEN IN THE DESERT. . .

"I like to wake up in the morning with a cup of coffee and a good devotional book. This book I can say is a good one: personal, practical and inspirational. You will feel yourself drawn in by the challenges the author faced. Her faith enabled her to grow even in her most difficult experiences and places in life. I highly recommend *Green in the Desert*. You will find it timely truth for your own spiritual journey."

Don Wilkerson

Co-Founder of Teen Challenge International

"I recommend this book to you because I can without reservation recommend its author. C.J. Reynes is a friend, colleague, and mentor whom I respect and have trusted for over 25 years. Truth can be hard or honeyed and in season we need it to be both. C.J. speaks hard truths prophetically and honestly out of a honeyed, loving, and joyful heart. *Green in the Desert* is transparent and timely. I hope you enjoy it as much as I have."

Dick Brogden

Co-Founder of Live Dead Saudi Arabia, August 2020

"James urges us to 'count it all joy when you meet trials of various kinds.' The good news is that you and I will never run out of such opportunities!"

"Ten chapters, ten compelling scary, painful or traumatic events are sifted from C.J.'s past, including three decades of life on the frontlines of ministry in China and the Arab Gulf. She then skillfully weaves in personal narrative, Scripture, and frank discussion of how we can grow. The lessons are applicable to all who yearn to walk in footsteps of faith. You will enjoy this book!"

Daniel Sinclair

Author of "A Vision of the Possible: Pioneer Church Planting in Teams"

Nineteen years Field Director with Frontiers

GREEN IN THE DESERT

GET HOPE TO SURVIVE AND FAITH TO THRIVE IN
HARDSHIPS

C.J. REYNES

MOF PUBLISHING

C.J. Reynes

GREEN IN THE DESERT

ISBN 978-1-777-6615-2-6

About the Author: After thirty years of living in the Middle East and China, C.J. Reynes brings personal experience and professional cultural intelligence certification to her life coaching. Her down home upbringing combined with international travel brings warmth and insight to the hope and inspiration she craves to give to others in her writing and motivational speaking. When not pursuing her career interests, C.J. likes to climb mountains, hunt for rocks and spend time with her mom, three grown sons and spouses along with her two grandchildren wherever possible but especially in Colorado.

Contact information: CJReynes@Patient-Endurance.com

MOF PUBLISHING

DEDICATION

I dedicate this book to the glory of God. It is written with the expressed purpose of pointing people to Him and helping them to thrive in relationship with Him through Jesus Christ, our Lord. May the things I've experienced become building blocks of hope and faith for anyone who hears of them, bringing God even greater praise.

WITH APPRECIATION

I'm grateful for the multitudes of brothers and sisters in Christ who have gone before me, and from whom I have learned. I'm blessed by the eternal truths that the Holy Spirit has taught me through you.

I am blessed to have had several excellent, spiritual leaders and mentors. They've gone out of their way to invest in me. May your investment bring great dividends for our King, who has seen your labors of love.

Thank you, to my team of beta readers! Your help has been invaluable!

Last, but not least, I am most appreciative of my husband and children, my parents and siblings, along with all my relatives and good friends. The deep love I have for you, who accept me as part of your tribe, can't be expressed in words. Each of you have enriched my life and helped form me into the person I am today. May the joy of our Lord be continually and ever increasingly yours. – C.J.

CONTENTS

PREFACE
ALWAYS GREEN

"But blessed is the man who trusts in the LORD; whose confidence is in him. He will be like a tree planted by the water that sends out its roots by the stream. It does not fear when heat comes; its leaves are always green. It has no worries in a year of drought and never fails to bear fruit." – Jeremiah 17: 7, 8

Green in the Desert is a compilation of personal life stories that show how God has used my various hardships to build resilience and strengthen me. These stories will lift your spirit. Each chapter presents a *key*, a spiritual principle used or learned during my time of trouble, to help you lean on God in your own trials, or "deserts."

I liken unwanted struggles we face to being in a desert. Our difficulties, like the blistering sun and harsh winds blasting us with sand, are painful. Feelings of helplessness and discomfort can bring a sense of spiritual dryness, thirst, and abandonment by God.

In a desert, it seems impossible that anything can survive... let alone thrive. Yet God, in His wisdom, has made it possible for some plants and animals to do just that!

These unique wonders of creation that live in physical deserts give me hope in my spiritual deserts. Spiritual deserts are difficult times when it's hard to hear from God and you feel spiritually empty or feel nothing at all.

As God provides for the camels, lizards, and broom and palm trees, He also gives us the ability to thrive in life's dry and challenging deserts. His spiritual, living water is available to all who ask Him. The streams are there! They may not be visible to the naked eye... but they are there! We always have this hope.

We have hope to survive.

Praise God for hope! That's what this book is all about. Hope keeps our spirits alive long enough to strengthen our faith. When we feel faith start to rise in us, we can gain God's perspective on our situation.

Faith operates despite our feelings during painful circumstances. It is exactly when we feel like we can't go on that we can learn to trust God's promises instead of our emotions.

Despite the hard facts that we are dealing with, we can be assured God's truths supersede. This is what faith is all about. It's choosing to believe God's perspective is more real than what we see, hear, or feel.

We can, in the end, be thankful for our hardships. They help us to see God's marvelous love and intervention on our behalf. They can also strengthen our endurance level to trust God in ever-increasing measure.

As we journey with God through trial after trial, we eventually come to understand that it's possible to do more than survive. We can use our struggles to help us thrive spiritually. No matter what we face, we can recall the times God, in His faithfulness, has wondrously met our needs.

My deepest and most sincere prayer is that you will find these stories from my life's journey to be a reminder of God's faithful love. May they be an encouragement to you.

I'm an ordinary person, yet one who has learned my feelings often lie. I've learned that God has the final word about the events of my life. His written Word, the Holy Bible, is more than a "survival manual" for me. It's my *thrival* **manual**!

My friend, we **can survive** our hardships. We **can thrive** while still seeing no solution or way out of our difficult deserts. What God has done for me, He can also do for you. May you be encouraged with the fact that God is the same yesterday, today, and forever.

I bless you with hope and Christ's peace. May the enemy of your soul be bound and no longer able to discourage you with partial truths and lies. In the mighty name of Jesus Christ our King, I pray that hope and the gift of faith may be given to you in your time of need... in **your** deserts. Amen.

C.J. Reynes

1

FIRST AND BEST MIRACLE

DESERT OF DESPAIR

Thrival Key: *I Can Trust God's Perfect Love for Me*

WHAT AN UNEXPECTED ANNOUNCEMENT MY DAD MADE WHEN I WAS 15 YEARS old! He told me that our family would be moving, and **it turned my world upside down**. I grew up on the east side of Des Moines, Iowa, but found myself thrust into a completely different school district during my high school years.

Because my father was a high-school principal, he wanted me to have a better education suitable for college preparation. So, we moved to the suburbs where he worked. He became *my* principal.

Everyone at the new school was a stranger to me. That is, except for two brothers that I had recently met at our family's new church. They provided me with a small nugget of comfort for which I was extremely grateful.

I had only just met the oldest of the two about a week before school started. It was a most fortunate meeting, however, because he was the senior class president and a captain of the football team. Being kind and the popular guy that he was, he introduced me to many of his friends. It was strange to have so many people being friendly to me. This was not what I had become used to during my junior high years.

In my very first week of junior high school, I had an experience that dramatically affected my self-image. I was alone in the school hallway standing in front of my locker when a handsome boy—the one I had a crush on—came walking toward me. My heart began to beat faster. I couldn't believe that I had become the focus of his gaze!

As he drew near, he squeezed my chest and made a snide remark about its small size. Oh! The absolute horror I felt! I was stunned! ***My crush had turned into that which crushed me!*** I had been looking forward to being at "the big kids' school," yet instantly, my elation was turned to deep sadness as I joined the "Me Too" movement long before it existed.

As days went by, I turned inward, drawing away from other people and feeling awkward. I was often called "Twiggy," and I couldn't help but think about how ugly I must be. I didn't feel that I was good enough for friendship with anyone. To make matters worse, I quickly discovered that I could not understand algebra.

I came to school early every morning to have private tutoring with my algebra teacher, but even that didn't seem to help. I could barely get by. Algebra was so confusing that it felt like my teacher, Mr. Wilson, was speaking in a foreign language I couldn't understand. This made me feel stupid, as well as ugly.

In ninth grade, I happened upon a friendship with two girls who were also feeling sorry for themselves. One of the girls (I'll call her Molly) introduced me to a do-good young girl's organization. Though I thought its secret handshakes and walking paths around an altar were a bit strange, I enjoyed belonging to something.

The other girl (I'll call her Susie) had divorced parents. In the early 1970s, this was uncommon. Her dad was a hypnotist, and her mom could read people's futures with tarot cards and astrology charts. She was experienced in extrasensory perception (ESP), and we were eager to learn from her.

When at Susie's home, the three of us were taught how to "read" her mom's thoughts. I remember sitting on opposite sides and various corners of the living room with lights dimmed. We girls would write the thoughts that came to us while her mom mentally projected hers to us.

She wrote her thoughts down in advance to later prove to us what they were with each experiment. Afterwards, we would compare our papers. How surprised and excited we were to discover that the supernatural world truly did exist! We could actually read someone else's thoughts!

This was an exhilarating time in my life. In addition to ESP experiments, I learned about other supernatural activities from my Sunday School teacher. Though he was supposed to be teaching me about the Bible, he introduced levitation to us, as well as reading people's auras.

I didn't understand the source of this new and thrilling power I was experiencing, which proved to be a problem. I was an innocent victim of ignorance. Satan, the enemy of my soul, was delighted to take advantage of that which I did not understand. These activities provided an entryway for him to access my mind in ways he did not have before.

I later learned through studying Scripture that my supernatural experiences were demonically assisted. Though they were fascinating initially, I quickly began to feel that life had no purpose. I was in despair of ever having significance.

The other two in our trio began to feel the same way, and we exchanged our supernatural activities for doing things that made us feel sorry for ourselves instead. We would turn our black light on, play sad music, and discuss the "best" way to end our lives. **We couldn't see any purpose in waking up, going to school, being a "loser," and then going home to do homework, eat, go to sleep, and start the whole cycle over again.**

It was with this mindset that I entered my new high school. One girl, named JoAnne, realized that I didn't know anyone, so she made it her mission to befriend me.

It was October of 1975 when she asked me if I'd like to attend a small Bible study. JoAnne said that it would be very informal, so I decided I would see what it was all about. I really didn't have any big expectations because I had been raised with Christian beliefs, but I didn't feel my life had any impact from them.

I had attended Sunday school at the Baptist church when I was in preschool and had taken catechism class at the Presbyterian church near our home when in the seventh grade. While in high school, our family attended a Methodist church. It all seemed the same to me.

Like most good American citizens at the time, I believed that Jesus died on the cross for our sins. Our family went to church at least once a month and especially attended on Christmas and Easter.

With my former religious experiences, I had tried to be a "good girl" and meet the expectations of everyone. After all, my father, the high school principal, was also an Eagle Scout! I had to think about his reputation.

But, despite my best efforts, I continually felt I disappointed everyone. My purpose in going to the Bible study was to get to know JoAnne better because I liked the way it felt to be around her.

I honestly don't remember anything about the Bible study that night. I don't remember the topic or who was leading the discussion. But I remember the fact that we were told three of the students would be available to pray with us. They left the front room Bible study and went to a bedroom, awaiting any who wanted to be prayed for.

I will never forget going down the hallway leading to that bedroom. I wondered what would happen. When I arrived at the open bedroom door, I found myself voluntarily lunging down to kneel at the bed in front of me. The three high school seniors sitting there may have been surprised, but I wouldn't know because I didn't even look at them.

I vaguely remember that they seemed to be praying, but it sounded like gibberish to me. It wasn't English.

Though I heard this strange form of prayer in the background, I was only focused on talking with God. **I was desperate to surrender my life to Him, because I had come to believe that He loved me just the way I was.** I trusted that God's love for me was perfect and unconditional. I was only focused on Him.

When I was on my knees, without any instruction from the three, I raised my two hands toward heaven and said something to the effect of, "God, if it's true that You will accept me just as I am, I give all of me to You."

Though I grew up with the belief that Jesus died on the cross for my sins, this simple, intellectual fact had done nothing for me. I wanted to be accepted by Him. I intended to follow God with all my heart, whatever He might ask of me.

Instantly, I felt my self-doubt and self-loathing disappear. It felt as if a ton of concrete blocks resting on my head and invisible chains tied around me were demolished and fell off! Without understanding what was happening, I began to speak in "gibberish" language, too! I didn't know what was happening, nor how, but I knew it was from God, so I continued to revel in the experience. It felt so amazing!

I learned that night that God loved me and accepted me. He knew I could never live up to His standards without His help. I realized that this was the main reason Jesus came to earth in the first place. When I surrendered my life to Christ, the Holy Spirit came to live inside me, giving me His power to do what is right. I no longer had to rely on myself.

The sensation I had as His presence flooded my being is hard to describe. I didn't just have an emotional reaction to something spiritual. I was experiencing something that was tangibly felt.

He was the one who took me as I was. This was the beginning of my life as a new creation. **Without being told, I knew that my life now had purpose... I was a new and different person.**

When I left the bedroom and returned to the gathering that night, all the other students suddenly stopped talking and turned to look at me with gasps! They could see a visible difference in my face. One boy loudly proclaimed, "What happened to you?!"

For the rest of my high school days, much to my father's chagrin, I became known as the school "Jesus freak," a title that I proudly wore as a badge of honor. No one could get me to stop talking about JESUS!

There was a slogan for an evangelical campaign that year called, "I FOUND IT." Well, that was certainly true of me. I found eternal life and forgiveness of my sins through Jesus Christ. Though I didn't understand the theology of it all at that time, I knew I belonged to God from that time on. I was His. I knew this was good!

Instantly, I had an insatiable desire to read the Bible. After studying and devouring its contents for the first time in my life, I discovered that, actually, Christ is the one that found me! He came to seek and save the lost. I certainly had fallen into that category!

I'm forever grateful to the Lover of my Soul for seeing me for who I could become and not only for who I was at the time. He rescued me from my desert of despair, and you will see that He continued to protect me in later desert seasons of my life. Though He is enthroned in heaven in unapproachable light, by His Spirit, He has also become my most faithful friend!

THRIVAL KEY - I CAN TRUST GOD'S PERFECT LOVE FOR ME

"There is no fear in love. But perfect love drives out fear, because fear has to do with punishment. The one who fears is not made perfect in love." – 1 John 4:18

That night, while at the first Bible study I ever attended, changed everything for me. It happened when I finally understood that God's love for me didn't change based on how good or bad I was. I learned that His love for all people is unconditional. He greatly loves us no matter what we do, or have done. He *accepts* us as we are.

A favorite children's Sunday school song comes to mind. It says:

Jesus loves me, this I know. For the Bible tells me so.
Little ones to Him belong. They are weak, but He is strong.
Yes, Jesus loves me. Yes, Jesus loves me.
Yes, Jesus loves me. The Bible tells me so.
Jesus loves me when I'm good, when I do the things I should.
Jesus loves me when I'm bad, even though it makes Him sad.
Yes, Jesus loves me. Yes, Jesus loves me.
Yes, Jesus loves me. The Bible tells me so.

I SANG THIS SONG WHEN I WAS A CHILD, BUT THE WORDS DIDN'T STICK WITH me because I didn't realize I could actually have a relationship with God. He seemed so far off. I knew God was real and believed that He was good. But I also falsely believed I needed to be good before I could ask Him to forgive me and then experience His love and approval. Knowing I fell so far short of being good, I didn't think I had any hope.

I am so grateful that JoAnne invited me to that study. I learned that evening that I didn't have to change first, but that God would accept me as I was if I came to Him with a sincere heart. I could approach Him even though I wasn't "good." *He would then help me change* by giving me the power to do what was right in His eyes.

What freedom this gave me! I no longer had to perform or work hard at receiving approval from others. I had the approval of my Creator! I could now trust God with every detail of my life because He longs to forgive us. He loves us. He wants to help us when we are sincere about doing things His way and surrendering to His control.

This wasn't a problem for me. I had made every effort to live life on my own, with me being in control. **It wasn't working**. **I *wanted* God to have control of my life.** I found it easy to trust him when I experienced his love and acceptance. It was like nothing I had ever known before.

Choosing to side with Him, doing things His way and giving Him the reins of my life, was a "no brainer" at that point.

I believe that God's love for us all is perfect. It is flawless. It never fails. In fact, the Bible says, "God is love." It's who He is. Since His love is perfect, I can trust Him…always! This doesn't mean that I won't face hardships in my life. But it does mean that the deserts that God allows, He does so with my highest good in mind. He loves me and never leaves me.

As I've grown in my relationship with God, I've enjoyed studying the Bible continuously. It tells us that if we are surrendered to the Lord, there is never a time when we have a reason to be afraid. The book of First John says, "Perfect love drives out fear."

When I first read that, I believed it meant that I needed to have perfect love for God before I would stop being afraid. But just like I falsely believed I had to be good before I could approach God, I had this concept backwards too.

I've learned that I can trust God in every situation, even when I feel afraid. The reason I can do this is because I now realize how perfect God's love is for me. Understanding this truth and focusing on it, makes continuing in fear an impossibility.

It is not up to me to try hard to be perfect in my love for God. Rather, I must only choose to focus on His perfect love for me! Knowing Him and trusting Him… is how I am made perfect in love.

QUESTIONS TO PONDER: HOW CAN THE HOPE THAT GOD HAS PERFECT LOVE for you affect your life? What does accepting unconditional love mean to you?

PRAYER: LOVING FATHER, HEAVENLY HUSBAND, GOOD SHEPHERD, Dearest Friend, I come to You today with my hurts and concerns and want to ask for Your help in my life. Please intervene on my behalf. Help me to see my circumstances through Your eyes. Help me to trust You and to trust that Your love for me is working on my behalf. Help me to live a life that is surrendered to You. Thank You that Your love for me is perfect. Thank You that I never have to be afraid because You are always with me. In Jesus' name, Amen.

2

SNOWSTORM BREAKDOWN
DESERT OF DISASTER

Thrival Key: *I WILL Sing Praise*

I MARRIED MY HIGH SCHOOL SWEETHEART IN 1979, AND WE ENJOYED OUR young lives together for three years before having our firstborn son. Shortly before he was born, we joined a new church in a rural town 35 miles from our home in the capital city. My husband had recently been employed there, and we grew to love that town. There, we also grew in our love for Christ.

It was a blustery cold day in 1982, with frost on the trees and snow and ice on the roads. I had just picked up our son from the babysitter's house near the church. Enjoying the frosty artwork of nature in the country roads, despite the blowing snow, I praised God for his goodness.

Driving home alone with our son, void of anything but cornfields and distant farms, I was still 20 miles from our tiny trailer home when suddenly the car started to act funny. Unfortunately, mobile phones had not yet been invented.

I'm not a mechanic, so I don't know how to describe why I knew something was wrong, but I was greatly concerned we wouldn't be able to make it home in the bad weather. I didn't want to be stuck on the road, with no way to contact my husband while in freezing temperatures with our baby boy.

I wondered what I should do. I had no control over my situation. Nothing I could think of would improve my circumstances. I thought about our "spiritual parents" and tried to imagine what they would do.

I was grateful that God had blessed my husband and me with two wonderful sets of "spiritual parents." The pastor who married us, along with his precious wife, took us under their wings, and taught us how to follow the teachings of Jesus.

Since we were both fairly new in our faith walk with Christ, they instructed us with the basics about serving God. They modeled how to live for Him with integrity, no matter the circumstances, and we came to understand much about total surrender to the Lord. God knew these lessons were of first importance for us.

After joining the rural church, our new pastor and his wife became our second spiritual role models. We learned many things from them, but the most significant was the lesson about having *faith*. We learned we could utilize faith now in the same way that the people did as described in the New Testament stories. God's miracles weren't reserved only for that time so long ago!

We watched our second set of mentors live out their trust in God. They believed in Him for miracles in answer to their prayers. It was a normal way of life for them. As we continued studying the Bible, we wanted to trust God for the impossible, as well.

Every Sunday, at the end of the pastor's message, people went to the church altar for prayer. We literally saw miraculous healings as commonplace events during those times. This ignited in us an even deeper hunger for God. And God was faithful to feed us! He began stretching our faith by giving us opportunities to use it.

So, I was in that old, used car, deeply concerned we might be in a life-threatening situation. I knew I had a choice to make. I could continue thinking about all the negative possibilities of our predicament, worrying with fear, or I could do what I knew my pastor would do.

Putting myself in Pastor Buck's place, I realized I needed to start praising Jesus! I had learned that I could ask Him for anything, and I began to praise the Lord for His love and care for us.

Recorded in the Bible, Jesus says that He will give us what we ask for. He'll do this so that God, the Father, would be glorified. I dared to trust God at that moment. I chose not to *let* myself be afraid.

I started to sing instead.

I remembered the story Pastor Buck shared about how he praised God when he was on the way to be audited by the IRS. Pastor Buck praised God all the time! It just so happened that the man who audited him had been with him in the elevator and heard him singing.

When Pastor Buck went to the assigned auditor to have his papers looked over, the auditor told him that his audit was no longer necessary. He said that anyone who joyfully sings on the way to have their taxes audited has nothing to hide! Pastor Buck left, thanking God, of course. Remembering *his* triumph, I chose to praise God and thank Him in *my* situation too.

This didn't happen easily or quickly. But I slowly and willfully tried to focus on God *above* the circumstances.

I reassured myself by quoting scripture verses out loud. I lifted them up to God as if they were my own prayers adapted to my current situation. Soon after choosing a different perspective on my possible disaster, I began to sense God's presence. I don't know how to describe the feeling I get when I sense that God is directing me. Perhaps, some would call it a gut feeling.

I perceived that instead of driving directly to our home, I should go to the home of our mechanic friend instead. I reasoned that it was approximately the same distance.

Arriving at our friend's home, we were welcomed in. The mechanic's wife, Diane, gave us something warm to drink while her husband looked at our car.

Just a few minutes after he went out to inspect our car, he came back in with an astonished look on his face. He was absolutely beside himself. He said that I had been driving that car while the battery wasn't hooked up. He told me that it was impossible for any car to operate in the condition that our car was in!

He was completely baffled. I then began to share how I had decided not to let fear control me. I chose to focus on God being the one in control of my life. I shared how I asked Him to take care of me, and I sang His praise, thanking Him for his goodness.

Our mechanic friend, also a believer, couldn't stop shouting in excitement when he realized that a miracle had taken place. My faith "muscle" had one of its first work-out sessions that blustery winter day... and I'm forever grateful that it did!

THRIVAL KEY - I WILL SING PRAISE

"Be joyful always; pray continually; give thanks in all circumstances, for this is God's will for you in Christ Jesus." – 1 Thessalonians 5:16-18

Have you ever NOT FELT like praising God? During that snowstorm, I definitely didn't feel like doing it! But through that experience, I now understand how quickly our feelings can change.

I learned that nothing readjusts our attention to God and off of our circumstances faster than singing praises to him. My husband has regularly reminded me that God is worthy of our worship and praise whether we feel like praising Him or not. We are *not* admonished to thank God *for* everything, but *in* everything. We can always thank God that He loves us and is with us.

Not being a theologian and sometimes struggling with scripture memorization, I've developed a helpful system to remind me of scriptural principles and truths. I summarize doctrines into one sentence phrases that I can remember. When it comes to the issue of praising God and thanking Him when I don't feel like it, I start repeating to myself... "I *will* sing praise."

The reason this phrase really works for me is because it reminds me that my *will* is what's involved in giving God my worship. **It doesn't depend on my feelings**. God is worthy despite them at times.

Knowing that God is worthy, and because I love him so dearly, I choose to sing and thank God as an act of my will... *especially* when my emotions don't agree. They become irrelevant.

We will be spending eternity praising God. The angels around the throne of God in heaven never stop, saying, "Holy, holy, holy!"

It's recorded in the Old Testament that the children of Israel had singers and worshippers in front of them in the procession of God's sanctuary. They asked for God to summon His power and show them His strength while they were mindful of the battles they faced with God's enemies (Psalm 68). This not only had the psychological effect of encouraging those who fought, but it also had spiritual significance.

God says in the Bible that He wants us to come into His presence with thanksgiving in our hearts. He wants us to give Him praise. He longs to receive the honor that is due Him.

When we praise the Lord sincerely from our hearts, I've learned it opens the door for God to pour out his blessings on us. It becomes a win-win situation. God is blessed by our praise, and we are given a double blessing.

I say "double blessing" because simply the act of drawing near to God gives us the sense of His presence, with the emotional warmness of intimacy with our Creator. On top of that, our bond with the Lord makes

Him want to bless us. To me, I think of it much like a very pleased parent who loves to dote on their kids when they take time to cuddle with them and sit on their laps.

Observing for myself how beneficial praising God has been, I've made it my default in the midst of even the worst situations or deserts I've had to face. It's what God wants, and it's also good for us. It helps us to change our gaze to that which matters in eternity. It's impossible to have a pity party with heaven as our focus.

Knowing that we will be worshipping God in heaven for all eternity, and that it's His will, *and* it's what's best for us, makes doing it a no-brainer! I can't go wrong by praising God.

I'm so grateful this is one of the first "thrival keys" I learned in my relationship with God. It has sustained me throughout my entire life and continues to do so.

I don't know who to credit for the quote that I've copied down on the inside flap of my Bible, but it is one of my favorites! I share it with you in the hope that it will encourage you as much as it has me.

"The deepest level of worship is praising God in spite of the pain, thanking God during the trials, trusting Him when we're tempted to lose hope, and loving Him when He seems so distant and far away. At my lowest, God is my hope. At my darkest, God is my light. At my weakest, God is my strength. At my saddest, God is my comforter." – unknown

I can't speak of praising God without also inserting one of my favorite praise songs. I use this song *especially in times when I have unhealthy, negative emotions.*

"I will sing praise! I will sing praise! No weapon formed against me shall remain. I rejoice, I will declare, God is my victory, and He is here! All of my life, in every season, You are still God; I have a reason to sing. I have a reason to worship!"

I *will* sing praise!

QUESTIONS TO PONDER: IN WHAT WAYS HAVE YOU EXPERIENCED THE blessings of praising God when you didn't feel like it? How could you make praising God your default reaction in every situation?

PRAYER: Lord, we come before Your presence today, choosing to give You praise. You are worthy! You are All-Powerful, All-Knowing, Ever Present, and You always do what is right. You've proven Your love to us by sending Your Son Jesus Christ to take the punishment each of us deserve. Thank you, Lord, for Your amazing love and grace. Help us to think of praising You more often than we do. Help us to choose to praise You instead of complaining and grumbling when we face unwanted pain in our lives. You are always worthy, and we want to make it our choice to rejoice in our relationship with You. I will sing praise to You, Lord. I choose to side with You against my old nature to do it. I don't want to ever rob You of glory that You could have through me. In Jesus' name, Amen.

"He turned the desert into pools of water and the parched ground into flowing springs..." – Psalm 107:35

Both photos © C.J. Reynes

3

CAN'T BREATHE

DESERT OF POSSIBLE DEATH

Thrival Key: *God Is FOR Me*

"I CAN'T BREATHE!" I WOKE MY HUSBAND WITH THESE WORDS IN SEPTEMBER of 1985. We were living in Rockford, Illinois because my husband's new job had brought us there. Earlier that day we gave a huge celebration for our second son's first birthday.

Over 200 people were invited, mostly the choir and orchestra members at our church. My husband directed these groups, and we felt quite close to them. Since none of our relatives lived in Illinois, they were the closest thing we had to family living nearby.

Under normal conditions, preparing an open house party for so many would be exhausting. So, you can imagine how depleted I was being three months pregnant. To top it off, I had just driven six hours that morning, returning to Illinois from a visit in Iowa.

Needless to say, my energy tank was on empty. But I had been determined to give our son an amazing birthday celebration. We had a wonderful party that night, though I think I was asleep before my head hit the pillow. I was thrilled that everything had gone so well!

The next thing I knew, I was suddenly awake and gasping for air. The pain in my lungs felt like a knife was stabbing me with each breath! No explanation was necessary when I woke up my husband. I needed medical attention immediately.

We headed for the emergency room after dropping off our children at a friend's home. When I was finally seen by the doctors my problem became more severe when they asked me to lie back. I screamed in pain and could only get relief to breathe if I sat straight up.

The doctors were quite puzzled. They admitted me to the hospital and kept me off food in case they needed to do emergency surgery. **Hearing this was a bit scary, to say the least!** Not even the doctors knew what was wrong. This was not reassuring. I didn't have time to think about it though, because I could hardly speak. I only knew that I needed to breathe and that I was exhausted.

Though I was in a desert of possible death, I had a deep inner peace despite the scary news. Of course, I was concerned, but I just had a "knowing" that **God was for me**. One way or another, I reasoned, I was going to be okay.

The first night in the hospital, I slept while sitting up. I was thankful to have had some rest. The following day I had many visitors. This was because my husband was on the staff of a church with 5,000 members. I was grateful for fellow believers who came to show their love and concern.

However, after the hospital staff saw all my visitors, they decided I could only be visited by the church pastors. Then they discovered our church had 17 pastors on staff, so they further limited my visits. Only the senior pastor was allowed to see me. The doctor said that I was in desperate need of rest.

I entered the hospital on a Thursday evening and stayed through the weekend with hopes of being discharged on Sunday afternoon. Since my symptoms had subsided, the doctors decided I must have had a case of pleurisy.

This, they explained, is a condition where the lining of the lungs gets inflamed and causes pain anytime the lungs touch them. They felt pleurisy was brought on due to lack of rest while pregnant, coupled with the long car drive.

On Sunday morning, I was excited about the prospect of getting out of the hospital, going home, and eating again. But it was not to be. While awaiting my release, I had another breathing attack and the pain was unbearable. I leaned forward as much as possible to try to suck in some air... all the while searching blindly behind me for the call button. I kept grabbing aimlessly to find it, but it was nowhere to be found!

While leaning forward, I could see the nurses' station just outside my door. One of the staff pastors from our church was there. He was in a heated debate with the nurse, who was refusing to let him visit me. When I saw him, I somehow had the strength to scream, "Get him in here!"

My friend, Dale, came into the room and immediately spoke out loud as if he was an ambassador of Christ's. He forbade Satan's attack on me, declaring that I was protected by the blood of Jesus.

He used Christ's authority to speak life into me, binding any of the devil's work. Instantly, the pain ceased, and I could breathe normally. I was very grateful for the tremendous sense of relief that followed.

The awesome power that faith-filled believers can have using the name of Jesus Christ is indescribable! "The prayer of a righteous person is powerful and effective," the Bible says. I found myself right smack in the middle of an object lesson that proved it.

The doctors couldn't find anything wrong with me after that, so they reluctantly released me after I signed a form and acknowledged my need for rest. They made me promise to discontinue my many responsibilities at church during the pregnancy.

I was then sent home, only to discover the full story surrounding my incident...

On the Friday night following my hospital admission, several of our choir members visited a church that had special revival meetings. The speaker operated in the spiritual gift called word of knowledge, a gift that enables people to know facts no man has told them. He also had the gift of prophecy, which is foretelling the future or giving utterances from God.

After this man finished his message, he pointed to the seats where several choir members were sitting. Then he said, "The devil is going to try to kill your pastor's wife, but God is not going to allow it." I'm so thankful that God truly cares for his children. He is the One who will always have the last word in any given situation.

Another part of this story is that our church was full and having four services every Sunday. We had three in the morning and one in the evening. With 17 staff pastors, they took turns sitting on the platform with our senior pastor.

The Sunday of my hospitalization, it was the College and Career Pastor's turn. Dale was seated behind the senior pastor and listening to his Sunday message. Suddenly, the Holy Spirit interrupted his thoughts and told him to go to the hospital to visit me.

When Dale heard the Spirit speak to him, he thought he would visit me after the service was over. His duty of sitting on the platform would then be completed. But the Holy Spirit interrupted his thoughts and once again spoke to him. He told him to stand up and immediately leave the platform to visit me. This, he did.

When I leaned forward, trying to call the nurses for help, I was more grateful than words can express to see Dale just outside my door. **I'm so thankful** for people who know how to listen to **and** obey the voice of the Holy Spirit!

I don't know what would have happened that day if Dale wouldn't have been obedient. I *do* know that sometimes our decisions to obey or *not* can be a literal matter of life or death. I was quite sobered by that thought, and I have tried to be obedient to the slightest whisper of the Holy Spirit ever since.

I, for one, am appreciative of believers who understand this principle, and who serve God above any fears of what men will think of them.

Dale must have wondered what the congregation would be thinking when they saw him walk out in the middle of our senior pastor's sermon, but he feared God and knew he had to obey.

God, please bless my friend Dale today. In Jesus' name, Amen.

THRIVAL KEY - GOD IS FOR ME

"If God is for us, who can be against us? For I am convinced that neither death nor life, neither angels nor demons, neither the present nor the future, nor any powers, neither height nor depth, nor anything else in all creation will be able to separate us from the love of God that is in Christ Jesus our Lord." – Romans 8:31, 38-39

To think that the Creator of the Universe actually cares about me and knows me by name is sometimes hard to grasp. Most of us would like to believe this is true, though we would have to admit that we don't always feel this.

We see so much evil in our world. We think, "If God has allowed bad things to happen to good people, how could I dare to think he would ever be **for** me?"

Even if we believe the theology that God has given humanity free will and acknowledge that evil exists due to man's free will, we have questions. We wonder how we could dare think God would be on our side.

There are many theological answers to this question. Though I'm not a theologian, I do know that having a relationship with God makes all the difference in the world!

When we lived in China, if someone had *guanxi* with another person, it meant they had "connections." They were then able to get permission to do things that others couldn't. In the Arab world, the word is *wasta*. In Bible terms, we call it "favor."

I once heard an illustration about a young boy who wanted to talk with the president of the U.S. He went to the gate of the White House and told the guard that he had a problem and wanted to see President Lincoln.

The guard told the young boy, in no uncertain terms, that his request would be impossible. He even chuckled at how naive the lad was until he discovered that the boy was the president's son! His relationship to the president gave him access. His relationship gave him favor.

The same is true with God. Having a relationship with Him allows us access that others do not have. When a person chooses to come under God's protective roof by submitting to Him as their Lord, He has promised to be there for us!

Though He cares for the whole world, we have become more than just His created beings. We have become part of His eternal family. We have become His sons and daughters. Oh, what a difference a relationship with God makes!

Whenever we find ourselves in desert situations that feel life-threatening or scary, all we must do is remind ourselves that the God who rules over all things has our backs. Our exact steps are ordered by Him.

He knew that we would be in that scenario, at that precise time, and He didn't prevent it. These are the perfect times for me to remember that *God is for me*. God is for us.

GOD is for me. Wow! He is the One who spoke the universe into existence and has no beginning or end. The All-Powerful, Omniscient One is backing me up. I couldn't ask for anything better!

If I were on a game show where I could phone a friend for help, who better to choose than the One who has all the answers? How much more so when we are in life's deserts. When we belong to Him, He takes care of us.

God **IS** for me. He is in the now… with me presently. This means that at any moment in time, no matter what I'm facing, God is with me. The moment I need Him, He is always there.

He's not just a God of the past who was. He's not just the God that will help me in the future. He exists eternally and is for me now. There is no doubt about it. He *is* actively involved in my life.

God is **FOR** me. He *wants* to bless me. He loves me as much as He loves Jesus. He wants to work everything together for my good. Even when we face awful circumstances, we can be assured our good God wants what is best for us. Trusting this as truth brings amazing inner peace.

God is for **ME**. Though God loved the world so much that He sent His Son to die for us, He desires individual relationships with each of us. There is no one person that Jesus did not come to die for. Even me.

God is for me because I am His child, and He blesses me based on my relationship with Him. I don't deserve His unconditional love. None of us do. Yet, I embrace all the love He has for me. It brings me a joy that nothing else can duplicate. He knows my name!

This had been especially true in situations that caused me to think, "This could be it! This could be the day that I die." Knowing God is for me, calms me. Remembering He has promised never to leave me makes everything all right, even in desert conditions.

This doesn't mean I don't see the reality of my trials. It means I choose to look above my hardships to see that God is much bigger. Corrie Ten Boom, the famous Nazi death camp survivor, said, "There is no pit so deep that God is not deeper still."

For me, it's like a scene in the movies where a small child is being bullied by a mean kid, when suddenly the kid runs away. The child wonders why he was saved until he turns around and sees his big brother showed up!

Jesus Christ is *our* Big Brother... and He always shows up for us when we need Him!

QUESTIONS TO PONDER: WHO HAS HAD YOUR BACK IN TIMES PAST? WHAT would keep you from believing *God* is for you and is totally reliable?

PRAYER: Thank You, Lord, for creating me because You want me to know You and be known by You! Thank you, Lord, that I can, at any moment, remind myself that *You are for me* because I belong to You. I choose to surrender my every care to You and rely on You. I choose to go to You first and trust You above my own ability to solve my problems and trials. I choose to be vulnerable with You, knowing that You will never let me down. Thank you, Lord, that I get to spend eternity with You and that this earthly existence is only a testing ground to allow us to choose life with You. In Jesus' name, Amen.

4

ACCUSED OF BEING SPIES

DESERT OF INTIMIDATION

Thrival Key: *Feelings Can Lie, God Never Does*

FIVE YEARS AFTER OUR THIRD SON WAS BORN, OUR FAMILY ARRIVED IN Northeast China in the windy, cold winter of 1991. We were so thrilled to finally have reached our goal that the extreme temperature of negative 25 degrees didn't dampen our excitement one bit.

My husband had accepted a job to teach English to university students there. We had heard they were eager to learn, and we were trusting for many opportunities to share our lives with them.

Though we were in a city of six million people, it was easy to find the U.S. Consulate to register our presence there. It was located just a 15-minute bicycle ride from our college.

Within our first week, we were surprised to get a call from the American Consul General (CG) himself. He generously offered to take us out to eat. It was an invitation that we were honored to have, and we quickly accepted it!

We soon discovered that he had three young children. They were approximately the ages of our three, and the CG was eager for them to have American friends.

Ours were the only other American boys in the city at the time. His children had been quite unhappy without playmates, so, like a good dad, he thought our family would be a good solution to his problem.

It was comforting to have this American family welcoming us. They were extremely kind, as well as generous, and urged us to visit them often. That said, I remember thinking to myself, "No Way! We can't get too close to these people."

I thought about how long and hard we had worked to get to China. It took lots of faith and prayer, along with several miracles. I was concerned that if we spent too much time with the U.S. CG's family, the Chinese government might be more suspicious of us than they already were.

In 1991, there were extremely few Americans living in China. Anyone that gave up life in America to live there was thought to have ulterior motives. This was because it hadn't been long since the Tiananmen Square massacre.

The Chinese Government was being extra cautious with foreigners. It seemed this was especially true of anyone who had relationships with employees of the U.S. government.

I will never forget the night when we first met the CG's family. I thanked our newfound friends for the wonderful meal they shared with us and said a polite goodbye. Then I felt compelled to get back to our apartment as soon as possible.

My emotions were greatly stirred. I quickly ascended the stairs to our home, leaving the rest of the family trailing behind me. I was uneasy and felt alarmed. I kept thinking, "No Way!"

At that precise moment in the dark stairwell, I felt the Holy Spirit interrupt my thoughts. He spoke to my heart with a stern tone, saying, "Lay it down!" You lay down your reasons for why you think I brought you here. Become friends with this family."

Wow, I was greatly surprised by this! Beyond any shadow of a doubt, I somehow knew it was the Lord's voice and not another. Even though my desire was the opposite, I submitted to the Holy Spirit.

By that time, I had learned to bend my will to His. He was my Lord, and I chose to obey Him joyfully, even at times when I didn't understand. I just needed to be convinced that I was hearing God's voice and not another.

Instead of distancing ourselves from this family, we became friends and spent lots of time together. Our children enjoyed numerous outings, and we learned much about the Chinese culture from them. Our two families grew quite close.

We had the joy of openly sharing our faith with them. The wife, we soon learned, was also a devoted Christian. What a blessing it was to enjoy times of fellowship and prayer with her!

In addition to the CG's family, there were other American friends in our city. Most of them were Christian, English teachers at universities. It was wonderful to have fellowship with people who understood our hearts so well. I made a habit of joining in early morning prayer with two of them daily.

One day before sunrise, while riding my bike to prayer, I had the sensation that I was being followed. I couldn't prove it, but I greatly sensed it. This was quite alarming to me because we had heard of several people who had become paranoid after moving to China.

At the prayer meeting, I shared my concerns with the other ladies. One of them had become a close friend with the foreign affairs officer at her college. She proceeded to tell me that I was not crazy! Her friend had just advised her not to be seen with me. She did this out of concern for her reputation.

She said the Chinese government sent a letter to all the universities and colleges in our province. It named our family as American spies. They were told not to associate with us.

What a shocker! I couldn't believe what I was hearing! I thought, "This is the stuff movies are made of!" It was so surreal!

When I returned home from prayer that morning, I had another surprise. I discovered our family had just been notified that our school was releasing us from our contract with them.

We were being forced to leave at the end of the spring semester. The reason, we were told, was because the college lacked enough funds to continue having a foreign teacher.

One really doesn't know how to prepare for these kinds of things. Our family had just sold all our earthly belongings. We had purchased one-way tickets to teach in China and had only been there for a few months.

Though our employment had been arranged by an educational sending agency, we were now being told we couldn't stay. We went to Beijing to talk with a leader of the agency. We hoped he might be able to get us a contract somewhere else.

While at his home, at the exact time we were visiting his family, the leader of our sending group received a phone call. Our college in the Northeast was requesting another teacher for the fall semester. Our friend very wisely inquired about why they were making such a request.

He curiously asked, "What happened to the family our educational agency just sent you?" The college responded with a lie. They said we had decided not to stay. They lied to save face, since saving face is one of the most important values of our Chinese friends.

We tried to apply at other colleges or universities in the area, but no one was willing to consider us. Being desperate and feeling quite intimidated by our desert circumstances, we took our need to the Fellowship.

This was a group of believing teachers and their families in our city that came together weekly to worship God. We packed more than 20 people in a student dorm room at the medical college. Our times together were always a great encouragement.

It was worth the 45-minute bicycle ride, even in the dead of winter. The best part about the Fellowship was our prayer meetings. Every time we agreed together about something, God answered. We saw so many prayers answered that it became our expected norm.

After we prayed, we waited to see how God would supply for our needs. We only had a few days left before our visas were to expire. We had no money to buy airplane tickets, and I was tempted to be afraid. I was tempted to let my mind wander with "What if . . ." scenarios that did not have happy endings.

The practical side of me had started to consider how we would buy food. Where would we live? Would we be imprisoned, living in China without money, no visa, and no means to fly home? What would happen to our three precious little sons?

I knew I couldn't allow the temptation of fear to take root in my heart. Despite what my eyes were seeing, what my ears were hearing, and what my feelings were telling me, I knew I had to trust God**. I had learned through experience that my feelings could lie, but He never does**. We strongly sensed the Lord wanted us to be in China, but we had no way out of our predicament. Intimidation from the massive control of the Communist Party started to overwhelm me; I knew I needed to change my focus.

When negative emotions were strong, I had discovered that I just needed to talk with my Savior and continue to give my concerns to Him. While in prayer, after God adjusted my perspective, He gave me the faith to believe this statement: "If God wants us to stay in this city, then the entire Chinese government won't be able to kick us out!"

This became my declaration. I shared it with the other believers who prayed this with us, trusting God to intervene. We then continued to wait.

During this desert of intimidation and testing of our faith, we received a phone call from the CG. He told us the main university of our city (an equivalent of an Ivy League School in the U.S.) requested we go to their Foreign Affairs Office to inquire about a job.

We were amazed and delighted by this news. Without hesitation, we went. Upon arrival, we were eagerly greeted by the university staff.

They gave contracts to both my husband and me for the upcoming year. We were absolutely elated and rejoiced that we were going to be staying in China! Suddenly our prayers were answered! Yet, we were perplexed and wondered how the university had heard of us.

At our earliest opportunity, we asked the CG about the incident. He proceeded to tell us he had visited the university, giving them a copy of my husband's resume. Before he left his meeting, he mentioned our children were the only friends his children had in the city.

We later discovered, according to Chinese culture (one with indirect communication), the university wanted to keep the CG happy, probably because he was responsible for issuing visas to their traveling scholars to go to the United States.

It turned out that this "Ivy League University of China" was the only one in the city that wasn't answerable to the provincial government. They didn't receive the correspondence with the orders not to hire us. Though we would never have dreamed of asking our friend to intervene for us, we were so very grateful that he did.

The following year, while teaching at Dong Da, we felt we were being thoroughly investigated by the Chinese Public Security Bureau. Much of this was verified through reports of our students. At this time, we had more practice not giving in to intimidation. We chose to trust God's words to us instead.

Thankfully, we didn't have any major problems with our visas after that incident. We were allowed to continue living there. Eventually, we assumed the Chinese government concluded we were not spies after all.

When all was said and done, we were truly able to say, "God works in mysterious ways!"

———

THRIVAL KEY - FEELINGS CAN LIE, GOD NEVER DOES

"…it is impossible for God to lie…" -- Hebrews 6:18

Intimidation was a common tactic Satan tried using against us while we lived in China. This was especially true in the early years shortly after foreigners were allowed in the country. Our spiritual enemy wanted to discourage us and make us quit. Due to constant surveillance, many English teachers in China had to battle with such feelings.

Students were required to sign in and out when visiting us. Things we spoke about in the privacy of our home were common knowledge to our Chinese hosts. Their careful watch over us was intentionally made known to us "for our own good."

We realized that if we allowed emotional intimidation to take root, it would cause us to fear. Fear would eventually paralyze us and keep us from being effective. Though seemingly impossible, God's grace enabled us to survive in that environment.

Handling the mental stress and keeping our feelings at bay was not easy. We could only thrive as we continuously chose to operate under our default of prayer. We cried out to God for strength and wisdom, instead of relying on our emotions. We learned that we couldn't always trust our emotions to line up with the truth.

Instead, we knew that God would never lie to us. We depended on Him and His written Word, the Bible. It lifted us above any intimidating feelings!

We are very grateful for being created in God's image and having the ability to reason and feel, but we also know that we will be in the process of renewing our minds for as long as we live. We don't always think the right thoughts. We don't always feel what God wants us to feel.

As humans, we base our thoughts and feelings on what we know, and our knowledge about any subject or situation is limited. Because of this, I have learned that my own feelings (and thoughts) can lie to me, but God never will. I can trust Him without reservation!

Was the government in China more powerful than we were? Yes. A hundred times, yes. But though this was true, God wanted me to lift up my eyes and focus on Him. He told me the whole truth…He was for me, and He is more powerful than any man or organization of man on the face of the earth.

Once I quit trusting my own senses and began to ask God about my circumstances, my life was forever changed. I was set free! My feelings no longer have control over me. Instead, I control them, by God's grace and the help of His Holy Spirit. I now trust Him to tell me the truth and give me His perspective in any situation.

Jesus wants us to go to Him when we feel weak or have burdens and concerns. If we do, He promises to give us emotional rest. I have learned to do just that. Though, I confess that there are times when I'd like to do this more quickly. I give my concerns to my Heavenly Father.

He helps me when I'm overwhelmed. He helps me when I'm afraid. He helps me when I'm sad. There is no time when I've needed His help that He hasn't been faithful to care, be there for me, and give me His perspective. He is full of compassion.

How wonderful to feel things from God's perspective! It's the most amazing and freeing thing that we can choose to do.

QUESTIONS TO PONDER: IN WHAT WAYS HAVE YOUR FEELINGS BEEN LYING TO you? What is stopping you from being honest about them with God and giving them to Him?

PRAYER: FATHER GOD, THANK YOU THAT IT'S IMPOSSIBLE FOR YOU TO LIE. Lord Jesus, thank You for being the Truth. We come to You, trusting that You will guide us through the help of Your Holy Spirit. Help us to trust You in our desert times. May we trust You above what we are feeling. If we are tempted to rely on something other than You, please remind us You are the only One who can truly heal our pain. Thank You, Lord, for coming to earth as a man. Though You were tested in every way, You never sinned and are now able to help us in our times of need. Thank You for loving us so deeply. We commit our heartaches and struggles to You. We ask You to help us focus on Your truth instead. In Jesus' mighty name, Amen.

Photo © C.J. Reynes

*"...they did not thirst when He led them through
the deserts..." – Isaiah 48:21*

5

BEING SUED

DESERT OF UNCERTAINTY

Thrival Key: *What's the Worst that Can Happen?*

"BAM, BAM, BAM, BAM!" UNEXPECTEDLY, I HEARD AN URGENT POUNDING AT our front door! Rushing to answer it, I found a Chinese woman holding her young, bleeding son. A small gash on his forehead caused blood to cover his face.

The woman was speaking quite rapidly. I wasn't yet proficient in Chinese, but I knew this woman needed help. While trying to understand the situation, our youngest son snuck around her at our entryway and scurried to his bedroom.

We soon learned more of what had just happened. The neighborhood children had been outside playing "King of the Hill." Debris piles left from recent construction on our campus provided the perfect playground for the group of five-year-olds, or so they thought!

Our son had thrown something down from the top of the heap. Unfortunately, it landed on the other boy's forehead.

Flagging down a taxi, I took the woman and her son to the hospital. While the doctors were working on the boy, the mother and I continued our attempt to understand each other.

We used a lot of hand signals and gestures. Unfortunately, the few Chinese words I knew were totally inadequate for the situation; yet we had found a way to connect.

After the boy was stitched up, I paid for all the expenses and repeatedly apologized for the incident. "Sorry" was one of the words I *did* know!

I was surprised and delighted to feel the warmth of this mother's gracious spirit toward us after that day. Despite the unfortunate event that brought us together, she wanted to be friends. The kindness of her spirit was evident to me, and I was very grateful.

It reminded me, once again, of the reputation our Chinese friends have regarding hospitality with strangers. We both felt quite happy as we sensed a beautiful friendship beginning.

Though our communication with each other left much to be desired, I had the sense that everything was going to be all right. I remember feeling deep contentment. My life had been enriched by this lady who was a stranger to me just hours before.

The very next day, however, our family was stunned to discover horrible news from our school's Foreign Affairs Department. Upon hearing of the incident with his son, my new friend's husband had decided to sue our family!

He had only recently left his guaranteed job with the Chinese government and had decided to "jump into the sea." This meant he relied on himself, not the "iron rice bowl," and was taking a chance at starting his own private law firm.

It appeared to us that this husband and his legal colleagues had discussed the situation and concluded we were "rich Americans." He apparently thought his family could benefit financially from his son's accidental injury. We were just what he needed to help his new practice!

This lawyer told the Foreign Affairs Office at our college that he was suing us for an astronomical amount! He said his son had plans to become a television newscaster when he grew up. Now that he had a scar on his forehead, his plans, and the income he would receive were gone. We were being sued for years of future lost income!

The Foreign Affairs Office of the Gold School said they would stand with us. They believed the lawyer's accusations and the amount of his lawsuit were unreasonable.

In fact, one of the school's head English teachers witnessed the entire event as he watched the children play. The head teacher assured us that the whole thing was an accident. He said all the Chinese children were playing together with our son, having fun in the same manner.

When the lawyer heard our school was supporting us, he said that he would sue the Gold School, too! He boldly said he wasn't afraid of them. After our college leaders heard this, they were sorry to tell us that they couldn't help us after all. They couldn't take the risk.

What were we to do?! We were planning on traveling home to the U.S. at the semester's end. God had miraculously provided the money; we had already purchased the plane tickets. Now, we were told that we could not leave the country because we were in the middle of a lawsuit.

Our tickets were non-refundable, and we were in a real jam. People were scared to be seen helping us in any way. They were all afraid of the lawyer. Fortunately, one of our former students had a dad who was a famous professor of law at the other Ivy-league-type university in our city.

Our former student secretly visited us, bringing helpful information from her father. She told us we were forbidden to tell anyone that he gave us advice. She said her father would deny helping us if he was asked.

She told us no matter what might happen, in a Chinese court of law, we would most certainly lose. "Foreigners always lose," her father said. He told us we must find a way to stop further action before it went to court.

Of course, we were reminded the Bible tells us the very same thing, and we were eager to comply! (Matthew 5:25)

We just didn't know how! Our circumstances were quite dire. We only had a week and a half before our planned visit to the United States.

We hardly had money to live on, having sold everything we owned just to get to China in the first place. We certainly didn't have the six-figure amount the lawyer demanded in his lawsuit. Not being allowed to leave was discouraging, to say the least. I had to fight feelings of fear and unbelief. We took our concerns to God in prayer.

We trusted that He would take care of us, though we couldn't see how. We also knew we needed others to help us in prayer. With great effort, my husband found a way to make an international call to our home church in the U.S.

His words on the phone didn't spell out any details because they were both fully aware that every word was being monitored. We were grateful that our pastor's wife, a spiritually sensitive woman, was able to understand his cryptic story and request for prayer.

That evening, as my husband and I lay in bed, we had a conversation I'll never forget! I'm pretty sure he must have detected some alarm deep in my heart because he was concerned about reassuring me.

With a question that sounded more like a declaration, my husband asked, ***"What's the worst that can happen?!"***

At first, I thought, "Are you kidding me?! Don't you understand how serious this is?!" But then, we discussed each possible scenario we could think of. We could end up in jail. Our children could be taken from us. We could even die in prison. After each possibility, my husband asked the same question again.

By the end of our discussion, we knew we had literally dedicated our children to God and trusted Him to take care of them. Then, we concluded that even if we died, we'd all end up in heaven with God forever.

Instantly, the atmosphere became peaceful because we were reminded of our hope of heaven. We were reminded that God is the One in control of our lives. He had proven Himself so very faithful to us over and over. Suddenly, we both declared out loud together, "What's the worst that can happen?!"

It sounds strange now, but at the time, we felt an unusual presence of the Holy Spirit with us. We *knew* God had sent us to China. We *knew* that He truly was sovereign. No matter what happened, we *knew* the truth and believed that heaven rules above everything else.

So, having absolute knowledge that our home church was fully awake and interceding for us, we fell fast asleep. We trusted God would, indeed, work this entire situation for our good. He would do it one way or another. All we had to do was wait.

The following morning, a different Chinese teacher from the English department, Gao, visited us, proving to be a true friend. He told us that he would go with us to the lawyer's home to discuss the issue.

Gao would act as a translator. We were a bit nervous about the idea, but eager to try to reason with the lawyer. We decided to attempt to settle with the boy's father in any way we could. So, off we went.

After we entered the lawyer's home, his wife and I caught a glimpse of each other. We smiled for a brief instant, remembering the friendship that had started. But the warmth of the moment was quickly disrupted by the awkwardness of her husband's actions.

We both lowered our eyes as her husband directed us into the main room of their home. Gao, not finding enough chairs, took the traditional Chinese stance of sitting on his "haunches." He was perfectly balanced, much as a baseball catcher is, and felt quite comfortable this way.

For the next hour or so, (though it seemed like an eternity), the lawyer proceeded to speak to us in Chinese. He rapidly blurted aloud, speaking on and on and on.

Each time he paused; he would then ask our squatting friend a question in Chinese. It was the only part of the interaction that we understood. He would inquire of him with a "Dui bu dui?" This, when translated, means "correct or not?"

With each episode of ranting, the lawyer followed up with the same question. Each time, Gao would answer the lawyer with a simple "Dui," meaning "correct."

We were totally in the dark. Oh, how curious we were about the conversation that was taking place! We wondered what the lawyer was referring to each time he asked Gao if he was correct or not.

All the while, I continued to have a peace. I was calm, yet feverishly and silently praying. God had blessed us with a deep faith the night before, and it was carrying me. In hindsight, I'm sure that our peace was a direct result of our church family's prayers back home.

Watching the whole discussion take place, I was suddenly startled and surprised. Gao stood up after one of the lawyer's pauses. He had a look of profound determination on his face that is imprinted on my mind. He then slowly began to speak. His words were firm and steady, sounding mighty and powerful with each carefully chosen word.

After just a few minutes of Gao's commentary, the most unexpected thing happened! The lawyer, standing opposite him, quickly covered his face, placing his head in his hands. The fingers that he had been shaking at Gao were now holding his lowered head in shame. He began to weep.

After a bit more hushed conversation, Gao told us the lawyer had just agreed to drop all the charges! We were quite confused, yet relieved.

We thanked the lawyer profusely, leaving his home as quickly as possible.

When we asked Gao what had happened, he ecstatically explained everything to us. We finally learned more of what the lawyer was asking each time he paused in his rantings.

The lawyer had asked Gao, "according to Chinese law," did he have the right to sue us or not? Was he correct? Each time our friend answered, "You are correct."

At the end of the conversation, when Gao stood up, he told the lawyer he had agreed with him the entire time. He agreed that according to Chinese law he was right. Then he said, "But according to *moral* law, you're wrong!"

He told the lawyer that he knew very well we had left a good life in the U.S. to come to help the Chinese people. He told him that we were a good family.

When the lawyer was confronted with the ethics of the situation, he felt ashamed. His conscience bothered him. He had been greedy. Never before had I appreciated the Communist Party of China. But in that moment, I was grateful they had taught against greed.

We praised God for this miraculous change of heart. We praised God for Gao, our newly trusted Chinese friend. We thanked the Lord for a man who didn't care about the pressure of the masses. Rather, he truly had convictions about doing what was right.

THRIVAL KEY – WHAT'S THE WORST THAT CAN HAPPEN?

"He will keep you strong to the end, so that you will be blameless on the day of our Lord Jesus Christ." – 1 Corinthians 1:8

Many times, when we are presented with tragic circumstances, our imaginations run wild. We think of the very worst that can happen. Usually, this isn't a healthy thing. When we picture the unimaginable, fear begins to grip our hearts.

Satan, the enemy of our souls, likes us to think about possibilities that petrify us and cripple our faith. He wants us to fixate on grim circumstances. He's delighted when we play scenarios of suffering and pain in our minds. He knows we will then lose focus on God.

How interesting that the devil is happy to point out dire possibilities and their consequences, but never finishes the story. For Christ-followers, people that belong to God, our stories never end where the devil leaves off...the rest of the story is Jesus. Jesus promised He would always be with us (Matthew 28:20). He'll never leave us or forsake us. Jesus tells us we are valuable to Him. He tells us the steps of a righteous person are ordered by Him. Nothing happens to us outside his permissive will.

If some of those scenarios come about, God has already given us His promise of provision. Should we face the unthinkable, we are told, "*all* things will work together for the good of those who love God and are called according to His purposes" (Romans 8:28).

Scripture promises us that no matter what happens, God will provide us with His grace, peace, and joy. We can trust that the One who's already proven His love to us will continue to care about us in our times of need.

Peace can fill our hearts when we view our circumstances from an eternal perspective. We remember God's goodness, sovereignty, and faithfulness. We remember that as our best friend, He has never failed us, and He never will. He wants what is best for us!

Donald C. Stamps, the author of the *Fire Bible*'s study notes, says, "Throughout redemptive history, believers have placed their trust in God even when it seemed as if all was lost. In such times, God gave the necessary faith and delivered his people according to his will and purpose."

When we find our imaginations running wild with negative possibilities, we can take our thoughts captive. We can remember that Jesus is with us, no matter what happens. He is our Good Shepherd.

WHAT'S THE WORST THAT CAN HAPPEN? SOME THINK OF SUFFERING. WHEN it comes to concern about suffering, I think of it as I did when anticipating childbirth. I heard it was painful, but I knew I could pray about it in advance and trust God to impart grace when the time came.

WHAT'S THE WORST THAT CAN HAPPEN? SOME THINK OF DEATH, EITHER their own or the death of a loved one. Yet remembering that the Bible says the death of God's saints is precious to Him, we can exchange our perspective for His. Scripture also says that we were created *for the very purpose* of having our mortality swallowed up by His eternal life (2 Corinthians 5:4, 5).

WHAT'S THE WORST THAT CAN HAPPEN? FOR TRUE CHRIST-FOLLOWERS, even the worst this earth can dole out ends in good news for us. **We have already passed from death into life.**

Living with an eternal mindset is how God wants us to operate. It's so liberating! It gives us the correct perspective, seeing our lives through His lens.

The next time you start to focus on the possibility of negative outcomes you might face, go ahead. Carry out the thought process to its *full* conclusion! You'll end up praising God!

QUESTIONS TO PONDER: WHAT PAST FEARS HAVE YOU ALLOWED TO CRIPPLE you? What could prevent you from trusting God's plan for your life?

PRAYER: FAITHFUL FATHER, THANK YOU FOR LOVING US SO MUCH THAT You sent Your Son to die in our place. We are grateful for the awesome privilege and opportunity to spend eternity with You in heaven. Please help us remember that You've promised this and that You never lie. Please help us to have Your perspective on death and suffering. Next time we are tempted to worry, please remind us that You will keep us strong to the end, if we surrender to You. In Jesus' name, Amen.

6

ENCIRCLED BY WILD MONKEYS
DESERT OF NO WAY OUT

Thrival Key: *God Never Leaves or Abandons His Children*

IN THE MID '90S, OUR FAMILY TRAVELED FOR THREE DAYS BY TRAIN FROM northeastern China to the southern tip, near the Hong Kong border. The train ride was a one-of-kind experience. We occupied five of the six bunks in an open compartment. People were walking up and down the aisle of the train at all times of the day and night.

I remember waking up to the sound of whistling. While rubbing my eyes to see what was happening, I watched the Chinese woman in the bunk across from me holding her naked infant, legs straddled wide over our shoes. She was potty training her baby with the sound of her whistle.

This ride is just one of the experiences we gave our sons, but I think an entire book could be written describing adventures found on trains in China. Our eyes, ears, and noses experienced new sensations continuously. Our whole family was filled with excitement during the trip.

No inconvenience would deter our exhilaration. We loved being together and learning new things about our Chinese friends. They were always kind and hospitable, and we learned a lot from them.

After arriving at the end of the line in Mainland China, we literally walked across by foot into Hong Kong. Wanting to spend some individual, quality time with "my boys," I told them I would spend a day with each of them. We would do whatever they wanted.

My oldest son, Brandon, was about 12 years old at the time and really enjoyed hiking. After asking around, we opted to hike at a popular public park situated at the bottom of the mountains. It was famous for having wild monkeys visit regularly. They would come down from the tropical, tree-covered forests where they lived and beg for food from visitors.

We planned to have lunch at the park before taking our hike. Pulling an orange out of our backpack, I intended to peel it and give a slice or two to the monkey nearby that had spotted us. But much to my surprise, the monkey didn't wait for us to give him a slice. He came running at us to take the whole thing! Being quite startled, I simply threw the orange at him and we got out of the way.

It was an exciting beginning to our anticipated hiking adventure. However, we soon discovered that the "hike" which had been highly recommended turned out to be a path that was mostly "man-made." It consisted of cement stairs ascending the mountain.

I love nature and was looking forward to something a little more rugged, but I tried not to let Brandon see my disappointment. We began climbing the stairs along with the crowd of tourists and local friends.

As we continued up the steps, we realized that the crowd of people was thinning out. Eventually, we were the only ones that dared to go as far and high.

This delighted me. I loved having some time alone with my son, and I used every minute of that special day to enjoy him and share with him about spiritual issues. Climbing to the peak, we had a blast.

Once there, we found what appeared to be a Buddhist shrine of some sort. I had heard and read a bit about them prior to our discovery that day.

I had a deep concern for the people of the region, wanting them to hear about Jesus Christ and that He was God's only way to having a restored relationship with our Creator. Believing that Buddhism was an anti-Biblical religion, I began to pray. **I believed I was Christ's ambassador and was there on my Heavenly Father's business.**

When our prayers were finished, I was full of joy and praised God that I had come to know that Jesus is THE TRUTH!

We sat for a while, enjoying the view, then started our descent. Since I had had many years of hiking and mountain climbing in the wild, I told my son we shouldn't use the man-made path. I even have a recollection of saying something like, "That path is for sissies!"

As we left the peak, we entered a jungle-like setting, surrounded by tall, tropical trees. It was as if we were under a huge green umbrella. The covering of leaves had beautiful tiny holes in it, allowing gleaming streams of sunshine to poke through. It was a beautiful sight.

About halfway down, we came upon an extremely deep crevice. There was no way forward, except to cross the crevice or go back up and find another way down.

Conveniently, someone had built a little eight- or ten-foot-long foot-bridge across the dangerous divide. Just as we were about to cross the footbridge, I paused and squatted down to point out a baby monkey I saw on a large boulder about 75 feet away.

As I pointed, the baby let out a high-pitched, blood-curdling scream. At that exact moment, I glanced into the treetops above the baby monkey and saw the branches far above our heads were packed full of adult monkeys.

I quickly scanned all the trees in the area to discover that we were surrounded by hundreds of them. Not one section was empty of monkeys for as far as I could see. We had walked right into the midst of them, unaware because of our downward focus.

Immediately, I realized the dangerous situation we might be in. Without having time to think, I heard a hissing sound. I looked to our left and saw a semi-circle of male mountain monkeys on the ground surrounding us at the bridge's entrance. An alpha-male monkey was in the center, standing about six feet away.

They had their arms raised and their fangs exposed. They were all about three feet tall. I glanced at the other side of the footbridge to see if there was an escape. But, across the footbridge was another semi-circle of male mountain monkeys.

Immediately, as both semi-circles were closing in on us, **I knew this was a fatal situation. We had no way out. It all happened so fast.**

In an instant, *without conscious thought*, I put my hands toward heaven and started to pray. The Holy Spirit started to pray through me. This was a time when my own words would have escaped me...

My body was on high alert. I now know what kind of an adrenaline rush happens to people in dire circumstances. If I had had time to consider our situation, the baby monkey wouldn't have been the only one screaming! Perhaps I would have acted irrationally? Perhaps I would have covered Brandon's body with my own, hoping to protect him?

We'll never know because in the middle of praying, suddenly, Brandon and I found ourselves on the other side of the footbridge, at least 50 yards away from the danger of any monkeys. Neither of us was able to remember how we got there.

We didn't have any recollection of crossing the footbridge. However, we didn't stop to discuss it! Once we found ourselves on the other side of the monkeys, we ran away, descending the mountain rapidly.

Some might think we must have crossed the footbridge, pushing ourselves through the monkeys that were intending to harm us. They may say we simply didn't remember this because it was so traumatic.

I've talked with Vietnam vets who've heard my monkey story, and they said that those monkeys in Hong Kong were the same kind they had encountered. I was told that they surely would have killed us if God had not intervened.

I personally think that God transported us to a safe distance away from the monkeys. It really doesn't matter to me *how* God rescued us. One way or another, we were miraculously spared. Whether by the miracle of supernatural transport, or by the miracle of shutting the mouths of the monkeys... God was watching over us.

I used this event as an opportunity to help my son understand that no matter what situation we find ourselves in, **as His children, He never leaves us or forsakes us**. We are never alone. We had just participated in an object lesson that proved the reality of this.

God's power, love, and protection for His children were unquestionably displayed for us that day! I will never forget God's amazing grace and how it felt to be under His watchful eye. What a Good Shepherd I serve!

————————

Thrival Key – God Never Leaves or Abandons His Children

"The Lord himself goes before you and will be with you; he will never leave you nor forsake you. Do not be afraid; do not be discouraged." – Deuteronomy 31:8

These words are some of the most comforting that we could ever hear. Especially in difficult times when we find ourselves with no way out, *we can always have hope,* knowing that God doesn't leave us.

Feeling alone, *whether by actually being alone, or just having the feeling* is quite possibly the most miserable sensation one could ever have, especially in a desert situation with no way out. Others could encourage us, give us a different perspective, or be of help in some way…if only they were there.

Worse yet is having people leave us in the middle of our dire conditions. What a sense of helplessness and pain there is in abandonment! Left alone, we are more vulnerable and easily subject to negative thoughts and emotions.

Most people will experience the feeling of being all alone. Whether toxic people have hurt us or good, well-meaning people have failed us, this reality remains. Many times, we are left alone due to circumstances outside anyone's control. Whatever the cause, if you've ever felt abandoned, it is not a happy place to be...

But what peace can fill our hearts, what security, when we are convinced that we will never be abandoned by God!

At the time we need Him the most, He's *always* there for us. This doesn't mean our circumstances will always turn out the way we would choose, but it does mean that Almighty God continuously cares for us and is there to help us. He uses methods that He knows are best for us.

If we are willing to humble ourselves and call out to Jesus, it ignites His heart into action.

Like a loving parent, God wants what is best for his child. Desiring for the child to learn new things, the parent gives his son or daughter space to grow. Yet, a good and loving parent is always standing by, if a cry for help is given. God is also like a lifeguard who immediately jumps into action when an SOS call is heard.

I'm so grateful that we don't have to pray elegant prayers for Him to hear us. We don't have to be perfect or especially religious. When we sincerely cry out for God's help, He loves to show up. This is especially true for those who call themselves by Christ's name, for those who surrender control of their lives to Him. He's got our backs! We can believe this is true because Jesus Christ told his followers that He would be with them always, and it's impossible for God to lie (Hebrews 6:18).

When I found myself in that dire situation with those wild monkeys, I was so glad that all I had to do was call for help.

There will always be times in our lives when we feel completely alone. No matter the horrible details that bring about our misery, it is in these times we need to remember that God won't ever leave us or abandon us. Remembering this can mean the difference between depression or being encouraged with patient endurance and faith. It could mean the difference between life or death.

I've been inspired by stories of Christians who have been imprisoned for their faith. Some friends, having been in solitary confinement, said they would imagine God was sitting on a chair in the prison cell with them.

Though they didn't have another human with them, they were not abandoned. They were not truly alone. They would have conversations with Him, and His presence was felt as surely as if He was tangibly there.

I long for everyone to fully understand that God loves them more deeply than they realize. He has concern for every individual. He knows them by name. God is love. This is not simply a cliché but is truth.

In our world, so drastically changed by COVID 19, my heart is saddened to hear of multitudes of souls who died without a single person in the room with them. It is heart-wrenching. I hope many of them knew this truth, and were able to feel God's presence with them, holding their hands.

I know that God wants everyone to understand how very wide and long and high and deep is the love that He has for them. I pray that you, the reader, will remember that *you are never truly alone.*

The God who created the universe and every good thing in it, created you. May you call out to Him in your time of need with complete confidence that He cares about you. May you give Him a chance to demonstrate His love to you, personally.

God's love for us all is so great that He sent His Son, Jesus Christ, to earth to die and provide a way of forgiveness that is just. Our Father God, who did not spare His Son, but gave Him for us, will also be there to help us in our times of need. We just need to ask.

He never leaves us or abandons us! Jesus Christ is with His followers ALWAYS.

QUESTIONS TO PONDER: IN WHAT WAYS HAVE YOU EXPERIENCED GOD'S HELP in a time of need? How often do you ask for and trust God to help you?

PRAYER: LORD GOD, OUR HEARTS ARE COMFORTED BY KNOWING THAT YOU will never leave us or abandon us. Thank You that You love us much more than the little birds You've created, and You've said that not even one of them falls to the ground apart from Your will. I am amazed to think that You know even the very number of hairs on my head. Help me to live in the safety and security that comes from knowing that You care for me and are always with me. Help me to bring You glory with my life. In Jesus Christ's name, Amen.

"The righteous will flourish like a palm tree . . .
they will still bear fruit in old age,
they will stay fresh and green." – Psalm 92:12, 14

7

GO THERE NOW
DESERT OF DEAD ENDS

Thrival Key: *There's Always a God Choice*

"OUR TICKETS ARE NO GOOD! AND THERE AREN'T ANY AVAILABLE ON ANY airline for the next two weeks!" This was the exasperated phone message we received from our departing American visitors.

We had just dropped them off at a hotel in Beijing after our four-and-a-half-hour ride to the capital city. Our guests had planned to take the hotel shuttle to the airport the next day for their scheduled flight back to the U.S.

Their paper tickets had said they needed to reconfirm *three days before* their departure. Our friends misunderstood and thought that they needed to reconfirm *within* three days before departure.

Our guests discovered their predicament after they arrived at their hotel when they tried to reconfirm their flights. They no longer had tickets, and the ones they had purchased were non-refundable. Unfortunately, our friends were inexperienced, young travelers. They were also short on money.

What were we to do? The only place to successfully purchase new tickets at the time was in Beijing. We were going to have to stay in the city to try to get flights for them to return to the U.S.

They didn't have money for an extended hotel stay, nor did we. To make matters worse, we didn't have any idea how long it would take to find a flight. Our young friends didn't speak any Chinese, and we were responsible for their well-being when in China.

Already being on the road back home, we turned the van around and returned to the airport hotel. We found a room at a cheaper place nearby and began to check out possible options.

It appeared our friends were being given the "rich American treatment." I hoped that after personally taking care of the issue, there'd be a way to purchase some new tickets.

Speaking Chinese gave me a huge advantage. I was a familiar face to many of the tourist spots. I had favor "in the bank" with many travel agents and tourist services because I hosted foreign guests quite often.

I used all the Chinese cultural knowledge and *guanxi* (relationships) that I had. This, along with my language skills, helped persuade the travel agents to try looking again for new tickets.

Though a thorough search was made, it was high tourist season, and no available flights were found in the computer system. At that time, the computers for China Air flights only listed upcoming air flights two weeks in advance.

We were really in a bind. That said, we tried hard not to show our deep concern. We told our friends not to worry, that God was going to provide. Encouraging them to eat, we said that we would be working on a solution to get them home.

Though we reassured our young co-laborers, when we got back to our own hotel room, I could feel panic start to rise in my heart. I began trying to remember where other travel agencies were in the city.

I thought that perhaps we might have more success if I tried looking elsewhere around town. As I started working on my plan of attack, I began to wonder if we should just head back to our smaller town and have them stay with us, indefinitely. Things looked grim.

It seemed as if that might be our only option. Due to the high tourist season, available hotel rooms in Beijing were quite expensive and hard to find. We were paying over $100 for our cheaper hotel that night as it was.

We could not afford to stay in Beijing for two weeks, hoping for a flight. The night's stay was already costing us much more than we felt comfortable paying.

When I started to feel the pressure of the situation rise up in my chest, I knew I needed to stop in my tracks and take the matter to God in *earnest* prayer. Though I had been breathing prayers all along since we'd heard the unwanted news, I needed to have an old-fashioned prayer meeting!

My husband had gone to a coffee shop to think and pray, so I had our hotel room to myself. I remember getting on my knees and leaning on the hotel bed. Praying while on my knees wasn't my habit. But somehow, in earnest need, I had the desire to kneel.

Even in desperate circumstances, I try to always come before the Lord with praise and thanksgiving. So, I attempted to offer a sacrifice of praise, but quickly dove into casting my burdens upon the Lord instead.

I speak with the Lord in the same manner that I speak with my husband or my best friend. So, I just started blurting out my concerns to Him. I say "concerns," but I'm pretty sure that they had crossed over into being worries instead.

I don't remember if I repented for my worried state or not. My faith was obviously falling short. But as I entered deep conversation with the Holy Spirit, I remember taking a pause to hear from Him. I was asking for guidance and wisdom, and I was expecting an answer.

In the stillness of the moment, I sensed God's peace and presence come over me. *I felt the Lord was speaking to my heart of hearts, saying, "Go there now."*

Somehow, I instinctively knew that I was being guided to go back to the same travel agent's office... now! I was convinced it was the Lord's voice, so I left the hotel immediately and walked about 15 minutes to revisit the same office that had just turned me away less than an hour before.

I had a confidence that something was going to happen, but I didn't know what. I knew I was going to look completely foolish to the travel agents. They had already made a sincere and deep search for tickets on my behalf. At this point, I had exhausted any favor I had with them.

When I opened the door, I could see the exasperated expression on the face of the lady behind the counter. I breathed more prayers, and God gave me persuasive and calming words while I pleaded for just *one more attempt* to find tickets.

Going way out of her way to assist me, the travel agent checked her computer again. She searched and searched. Finally, she told me that she was sorry, but that there were no available tickets on any airlines for the next two weeks.

I felt foolish and began to wonder if I had heard correctly from the Lord. "Was I just listening to my own imagination?" I started to get frustrated, and the peace I had felt was leaving me.

Before I could exit the travel agent's office, she excitedly said, "Wait a minute! Something just came up on the screen. There are two seats on a plane to the U.S. leaving the day after tomorrow."

Without hesitation, I said, "We'll take 'em!" I paid for the tickets, not knowing how we could afford them. Being grateful for God's amazing provision, I trusted He would somehow give us the money we needed.

I also believed He would cover the expense of just one more night's stay in Beijing. Oh! I felt so very valued by God to have Him answer our desperate prayers in such a spectacular way.

Seeing our friends off at the airport on the day of their departure, both my husband and I rejoiced and recounted all the times that God has come through for us. When we lean on Him so hard that we'll fall flat if He's not there... He always comes through! Praise His name!

THRIVAL KEY - THERE'S ALWAYS A GOD CHOICE

"She had a sister called Mary, who sat at the Lord's feet listening to what he said. But Martha was distracted by all the preparations that had to be made." – Luke 10:39, 40

"There's no good choice!" How many of us have been in that situation before? We just want to live a hassle-free life, and yet, we are often faced with options that make us cringe.

Perhaps doctors have presented us with a negative diagnosis and have laid out our alternatives. None of their choices seem good to us, yet we are told we must choose.

Whatever the conundrum, we like to find a good solution. We want to fix the problem. Yet, the fact remains that there are times when we can't do that. It appears that we must choose the *least bad* option... times when there is no "good choice" to make.

These are precisely the times when we need to remember **we always have a "God choice!"**

I once saw a Facebook meme with these words:

God has:
A better plan
A bigger perspective . . .
And I trust him.

If we are convinced that God may have an option that no human has yet conceived, *then* we'll be motivated to take our issues to Him. The key to obtaining the "God choice" will, however, require us to do our part.

Many of us, when presented with a crisis, pray and talk to God about our burdens, asking for guidance. What a wonderful privilege, to give our cares to Him! He doesn't want us to carry them ourselves. He knows that just one concern is too much for us.

But, after praying, we must choose not to worry about the issue any longer. We need to trust that God heard our heartfelt request and wants to work on our behalf. This done, we must realize that our responsibility is still not over. Our part in enjoying God's answer for guidance is twofold.

First, we must learn how to listen for God's reply. Even when we know better, we don't always give God the consideration we would give others after asking them a question. We don't take time to listen for His reply. He may want to say something to us at the time we've prayed. But we ask the Lord for guidance and then go off to figure out what seems best to us, expecting God to get our attention while we're on the move.

Most of us live in a world that expects action and results. We often hear others say, "Just *do* something!" But I have always been intrigued with the story of how Jesus defended Mary when her sister, Martha, criticized her. She was upset because she didn't think Mary was doing anything to help with the housework that obviously needed to be done.

What Martha didn't understand, however, is that Mary *was* actively doing something. Jesus said she chose what was "better" by sitting at His feet and listening.

Living overseas, I'm learning that it saves lots of time and energy when I choose to be still and give God time to speak with me. This is true even with simple, practical issues. For instance, it is often hard to locate specific products. If I need a particular item, I could go to many different stores and never find what I needed.

But when I take time to pray about my need *and then listen* for what God might have to say, I am often directed to the exact place that has what I'm looking for. It really is to my benefit to wait and listen.

While it's true that God is not obliged to answer us immediately, if I don't pause to listen, I'll never know if He wants to or not! **Too often, I don't expect an answer.**

Perhaps we think we must earn His favor first, or sometimes we are used to getting guidance from God in different ways. Truthfully, God speaks in a variety of ways. Yet, the fact remains that He likes to speak to us as a friend, if we will let Him.

I still remember learning the concept of "listening prayer." It absolutely transformed my relationship with God. A visiting speaker challenged us to start by taking five minutes every day at the end of our devotional time and be silent. During that time, we were encouraged to say, "Speak, Lord, Your servant is listening."

If, during that time, we feel an impression by the Holy Spirit, we were encouraged to keep a record of it, writing it down. On the other hand, if, during that time, I didn't hear anything from the Lord, then that was okay. God would be delighted that I was giving Him time to listen, should He desire to speak.

I started out with five minutes a day, and then I gradually upped it to 20 minutes a day. It's amazing how much God wants to speak to our hearts *if* we will just take the time to listen.

In silent times, it's much easier for the Holy Spirit to encourage us. He speaks just the right thing at the right time. His quiet impressions to my heart dispel dark and heavy emotional clouds.

I often sense the Holy Spirit telling me to "Listen!" That's the first requirement for obtaining our God choice.

The second is obedience. We need to be willing to pay the necessary price to carry out the thing the Lord tells us to do. We must be convinced, whatever it costs us, that God's solution is always the best one every time.

Unfortunately, we often choose to do things our own way, relying on our own reasoning and understanding. We aren't willing to be obedient.

We become like the Israelites of the Old Testament. We say we will follow God, but if the price is too costly, we convince ourselves that the Lord didn't really tell us to do *that*, did He? We rationalize and find a way of escape.

We do this by choosing what seems more logical to us. How interesting that the most logical choice to us is often one that leaves us in control. Our old nature prefers this, instead of being forced to trust God.

This brings us to the choice of denying our own desires, will, and emotions, and "putting them to death" *daily* in exchange for God's. Jesus Christ told us that if we want to follow Him, this is what we must do. Not to do it isn't a given option (Luke 9:23).

I'm amazed at how often we Christ-followers rationalize our own actions. We deceive ourselves, all the while using the excuse that we were directed by God. "After all, we prayed about it!"

Instead, if the impression we felt God gave us doesn't conflict with the Bible, then we should heed it. We deceive ourselves when we choose not to obey Him once we've sensed He has spoken.

When we act on what *seems* best to us, so often we are then disappointed, angry, or blame God when the outcome is less than desirable.

Some Christ-followers have fallen into this habit of living and have become disillusioned. They start to believe that God doesn't care for them, when, all along, He is longing to impart His tender-loving care.

If only we will take the time to listen *and* follow through on His instructions, we will experience His love. He truly does know what is best! ***When we follow God's plan, we have all of heaven's backing!*** Then, no matter the outcome, we feel at peace, knowing we listened to God. Next time you have a difficult decision to make and feel backed into a corner, please remember...

You always have a God choice!

QUESTIONS TO PONDER: How often do you give God time to respond to your prayers for guidance? What would prevent you from giving Him five minutes a day to listen to Him should He want to speak?

PRAYER: Father God, please forgive me for all the times I come to You asking for guidance yet go off to do my own thing. Help me learn how to listen to the whispers of Your Holy Spirit, knowing that You always want to communicate with me. Thank You for Your patient long-suffering with me as I grow to be more like You. I want to serve You with my whole heart, soul, mind, and strength. In Jesus' name, Amen.

8

SURGERY NEEDED?
DESERT OF DISEASE

Thrival Key: *Faith is Positional, Not Emotional*

"WE RECOMMEND THAT YOU HAVE A HYSTERECTOMY," SAID THE DOCTOR AT the Bumrungrad hospital in Thailand. Being "empty nesters," my husband and I had come out of China during our winter break to enjoy the warm weather. We also appreciated the quality medical care given at this hospital, so we decided to have a check-up.

The Bumrungrad hospital was the only hospital in the region that was accredited by U.S. standards. It has always been a big blessing to us, as they provide excellent service, are very thorough, and were about one-tenth of the cost of any similar services offered in the U.S. at that time.

On February 6, 2009, my annual check-up showed that I had a mass on my uterus. They thought it might just be a cyst, but the doctors decided I should have a hysterectomy as the best course of action. This would eliminate the need for a biopsy, and at that time in my life, they didn't want to mess around with other options.

I agreed to have the procedure, telling the doctors that I wanted to pray about it first. I said I would schedule the surgery three months from that date. But I made it clear that I would have the surgery *only if* they agreed to re-test me prior to the surgery and the tests showed it was still the best course of action.

The doctors were satisfied with this and the surgery was put on their calendars. Our medical insurance required that I receive pre-surgery authorization, so I filled in all the paperwork and they granted permission.

I was all set for the operation... with one exception: I truly believed that God wanted to heal me in a miraculous way this time. I don't think this was only wishful thinking, but rather, it was the sense that I had in my heart for this specific incident.

I couldn't stop thinking about the fact that I had asked God for a miraculous healing just a few years before when I needed shoulder surgery. God's answer at that time was to heal me with the help of the doctors and surgery. He wanted me to trust Him with the results, and He was training me in keeping my attention on Him above my circumstances. But this time felt different. I somehow felt I was going to be learning yet another new lesson from God.

I spent every day during the next three months praying and trusting that God was going to heal me. This was what I sensed He was asking me to trust Him for. I asked the Lord to allow the pre-exam to prove I was fine so no surgery would be needed. Our team members in China joined with me in unity, praying the same way.

Those three months passed quickly, and I boarded a plane that arrived in Bangkok late in the evening. Getting up earlier than necessary, I went to the hospital the next day with only a few hours of sleep. I wanted to arrive early enough to be re-examined before the scheduled surgery at 6:30 am.

When I arrived, no one there was prepared to re-test or examine me. It was assumed that I was having the hysterectomy that morning. The medical professionals tried, quite forcefully, to persuade me to have the procedure without further delay.

I have learned when it comes to living my life, choosing to function by listening to the Holy Spirit's leading, I should expect people not to comprehend my rationale. Most people can't understand.

I had a dilemma that early morning regarding how to show honor and respect to the hospital staff while insisting that I be re-tested before I submitted to having surgery. I see doctors as a huge blessing to society. I'm also grateful for the advanced technology available to us through modern medicine. Many lives have been saved and improved.

In fact, I even pursued becoming a nurse and I attended a nursing college. I appreciate the expertise of all professionals who have taken great care to attain the knowledge they have.

At the time, I reassured the doctor and medical staff that I understood they knew much more than I regarding my medical condition. However, I said they were making their best assessments according to the facts they had received three months prior.

I put myself in their place, appreciating doctors' concern and frustrations when it seems their advice is being ignored. That said, the doctors did not have the knowledge that I had regarding biblical truths. They did not understand, that in my own right, I was an expert in my personal walk with God and His Spirit's interaction with me. **These Buddhist doctors could not possibly grasp what I knew about listening to the Holy Spirit of Christ within me.**

And I did not expect them to.

The Bible tells us that spiritual matters are spiritually discerned (1 Corinthians 2:14). A person without the Spirit of God living within them simply cannot comprehend issues regarding how the Holy Spirit works. Expecting them to understand would be futile. It would be like trying to read a PDF file on the computer without having the right app to do that.

Though it is often uncomfortable to be misunderstood by others, I've learned not to budge if I sense the Holy Spirit is leading me. If I'm proven wrong, I'll embrace correction and sound thinking.

But at the time, I felt it was a very reasonable request to be re-tested before I signed consent forms for surgery. This was especially true since that was the condition I had agreed to. Unfortunately, with the resistance I was facing, I had to firmly demand it.

I had to be willing to be considered a fool to be obedient to what I felt God was asking me to do. I didn't make friends of the medical staff that day. But when I insisted on being tested, I had a "knowing in my knower" that it was what had to happen.

The way I remember it, the hospital could re-schedule the surgery for the following early morning. Thankfully, the doctor agreed to give me another exam and test that same day.

After the exam, I was re-tested and was told to come back the next day for the hysterectomy. The doctors were fully expecting to carry out their plan of action, though they had been inconveniently delayed. They were convinced the test results would say the same as they had three months prior.

Leaving the hospital, I went back to my hotel and spent the day in prayer. Committing the test results to God, as I had been doing in the previous months, I felt a quiet peace. I was stirred to give the whole situation to Him once again. I especially gave Him my desire not to have an operation.

I could have focused on the emotions I was starting to feel when negotiating with the hospital. The standoff with the staff brought up feelings of uncertainty and confusion. But I knew that if I did focus on my feelings, it would bring deeper frustration and doubt.

I knew that Satan wanted me to give my attention to the diseased uterus the doctors had found. He wanted me to fear for my life. I had many thoughts about one of my best friends who had died because uterine cancer went to her brain. The enemy of my soul wanted me to enter into a desert season and focus on hardships. Jesus wanted me to trust Him with all possible outcomes. Even in deserts, He gives living water to those who ask.

I had a choice to make. I could allow myself to think about all the possible negative outcomes the doctors presented me, or I could do what Jesus told me to do. He said that I shouldn't *let my heart be troubled or afraid.* He told me to trust Him.

As His daughter, He had given me many promises in His Word, and I knew I was dearly loved. My emotions, though real, were not more relevant than the facts of my relationship to God.

I told God that I would proceed according to the doctor's advice if the tests showed I still needed surgery. I believed He wanted to heal me, either way... miraculously or with the doctor's help.

The following morning when I went to the hospital, the doctor was a bit hard to read as he entered the room. I fully expected him to tell me the test results were good, and I no longer had any need for surgery. After observing him, however, a nagging thought came to me. *Maybe I was wrong and had misunderstood what God was saying in this incident. Maybe God really did want to use the doctors in this situation, after all.*

My doctor was slow to speak and used a very professional tone of voice. He told me the exam and test results showed no existing problems whatsoever. I no longer had any need for surgery! I'm pretty sure I gave an exuberant "Praise God!" as I'm in the habit of doing. But the doctor seemed unphased when he told me I needed to consult with him once more before I returned to China.

At the consultation, my doctor said he had no explanation for how things happened with me. Then immediately after this statement, I remember him asking me specifically, "Why are you in such good health?" Without thinking, I answered, "I pray a lot." He responded by saying, "Well, it's working!"

Those were the last words the doctor and I shared as I was leaving his office. I am so thankful that our Heavenly Father takes care of all the details in our lives. He knows the very number count of hairs on our head at any given moment. We are always much closer to His heart than it sometimes *feels* we are.

A few months later, I was contacted by the insurance company. They were following up and said they were concerned since they hadn't received the claim for the surgery, and they had given pre-approval. When I informed the insurance company the surgery was deemed no longer necessary, they wanted more information.

I was able to proudly proclaim, as a testimony to God's greatness, one more time, that Creator God in heaven, in answer to my prayers, miraculously healed me. It was proven with scientific medical tests!

THRIVAL KEY – FAITH IS POSITIONAL, NOT EMOTIONAL

"And without faith it is impossible to please God, because anyone who comes to him must believe that he exists and that he is the rewarder of those who earnestly seek him." Hebrews 11:6

Many of us have been in situations where we see someone really in need of a miracle, and our heart is moved. We may offer up a silent prayer for them, and then go about our business. But many times, I hear God ask me to be the answer to the prayers of that person. He wants me to pray for them. The question becomes, am I willing to partner with God at that time?

He looks for someone willing to be "His hands extended" to the needs of others. Though there are times when it feels uncomfortable, I often sense He wants me to go up to a stranger and ask permission to pray for them in Jesus' name.

God cares for everyone and sees our needs. He wants to use His followers to put our arms around hurting people. He wants us to share the Good News of Christ with them, so they can feel His love and know His truth. But one massive obstacle often stands in the way: our emotions.

I sometimes don't *feel* like I have the faith to pray for others. Or I *feel* like someone else would be more qualified. I often don't *feel* that my prayers would make a difference. I find myself asking God to send someone else to help.

I've been in prayer meetings where the question is asked, "Who has the faith to believe for healing?" Those who raise their hands are called upon to come and pray.

In those moments, I've found myself asking, do I *feel* I have enough faith to see that person healed? That question is quite deceptive. It is the wrong question**. I must remind myself that having faith isn't a matter of how I feel.**

I remember that the Bible says that faith comes from hearing the Word of God. It is something that we have or don't have. It is not a matter of how emotionally spiritual I sense I am. I must continually remind myself that feelings can lie to me. I can't always trust them.

There have been times when my emotions have kept me from doing things, even when I know I could do them well. If I listen to my feelings on the matter, I may not even try.

I've come to realize that one of Satan's biggest weapons against Christ's followers is to try to steal our faith. **He does this by getting us to focus on our feelings when we are in negative circumstances. If**

he can get us focused on them, we stop looking to God. We then give our emotions power to control us.

Instead, I must continually choose to yield to what God has to say. This has become a matter of utmost importance to me. I've realized it could also possibly be a matter of life or death for me or someone else! I'm not saying that any of us should deny that we have feelings or emotions. Rather, I've come to the place where I've just learned that they are not as trustworthy as God is. My faith is in Him.

When we spend time with Jesus and take the time to listen, we grow deeper in our relationship with Him. Just as in any relationship, the more time we spend with each other, the more we become like the one we are with.

Many times, I don't have to ask Jesus what He wants. If I have been spending time with Him, I usually will already know. I won't hesitate to pray a prayer of faith with someone when I know that's what God would have me do.

It isn't a matter of a feeling that I need to work up. I don't need to have some sort of special anointing to pray. But I do need to maintain an ever-deepening relationship with Him. The Lord often reminds me that I am a joint heir with Jesus Christ, as the Bible says (Romans 8:17). I am also His child, and He wants me to enjoy all His benefits. My faith is strengthened when I remember these things.

My husband and I have been married for 40 years and counting. The more time we spend together, the more deeply I've begun to think like him. I know what he likes and doesn't. Having a good relationship with him, I know not to order a Coke for my husband. I have faith. I know that iced tea without sugar or lemon and with very little ice will make him happy instead.

How can I have faith about this matter? It is NOT a matter of how emotionally sure I am. It is rather a matter of fact. Because of my position as his wife, I know full well my husband hasn't had a sugared Coke for decades.

Having faith in God operates much the same way. Knowing that I belong to God and spending time with Him, I'm learning the things He likes and dislikes. I know that He delights to listen to me and care for me.

When the doctor in Thailand wanted me to have surgery, my feelings were all over the place. Surgery can be scary! It was not a good feeling. I asked for time to pray, so I could hear from my Heavenly Father and understand what He wanted me to do.

After three months of seeking Him and listening to Him, I knew what He'd told me, what God and I had discussed. I had faith in what He said because I was in relationship with my Creator. When my desire to be re-tested before surgery was challenged, I chose not to let the feelings of intimidation control me. Instead, I chose to trust what God had said. I had faith in Him through our relationship.

Jesus said we should give God all our concerns. I like this. I like not carrying the weight of deep burdens. I have confidence my Heavenly Father will help me. He will answer my prayer IF I know I'm asking for something He would want in the first place. Whether I feel like I'm deserving or not, because of His grace, the fact remains that I've become His daughter. This is the only thing that matters.

When asking for an answer to prayer that seems absurd to others, I often remind myself of the verse, "You do not have because you do not ask God" (James 4:2). I remind the Lord Jesus that He said I can ask Him for anything, and He will do it so that God, the Father, might be glorified through Him. He wants me to ask Him for help.

Since Jesus told me I could ask for ANYTHING... I dare to do so with the faith of a little child. But I also remember that another verse tells us we have the condition of asking in accordance with God's will before we know that He hears us. I've learned to make sure my request is something He wants before asking. If I don't know for sure, then I ask Him about that first.

Being assured that the Lord desires to help me, it's easy to have faith that He will do as He said He would.

I have learned that this is the key. Knowing (or at least being convinced for myself that I think I know) that something is probably God's will for me before asking is what gives me faith. Secure in my relationship to God, knowing I am His daughter and have come to truly *know* Him, makes trusting Him easy.

Our Heavenly Father is GOOD! He is happy when we ask, and He delights to give us answers. When we wait for His answer before acting on something, we can walk with the assurance of His blessing. God can be trusted. He delights to bless those who rely on Him.

Whether or not we feel spiritual doesn't matter. If we've trusted Jesus Christ as our Savior and surrendered our lives to His Lordship, we have become His blessed children. Therefore, we can approach our Father in heaven with faith. Because of our position in relationship with

God we have favor with Him. This truth is made clear throughout the New Testament, and it is **more real** than any feelings we may have.

QUESTIONS TO PONDER: WHAT SITUATIONS HAVE YOU FACED, FOCUSING ON your emotions, rather than the fact that you are a child of God? What needs to happen for you to "know in your knower" that the promises in the New Testament are valid for you today?

PRAYER: LORD, GOD, I COME TO YOU TODAY, ASKING THAT YOU HELP ME realize all the benefits You offer me as Your Child. Help me to utilize the things that Christ's sacrificial blood made available to me... the things that You want me to take advantage of. Help me to know You more deeply today than I have known You before. I want to be like You, knowing Your desires. Please increase my faith. I DO believe, please help my unbelief. Thank You for being the embodiment of Goodness. Thank You for desiring to bless Your children. I love You, Lord. In Jesus' name, Amen.

Photo © C.J. Reynes

"...I provide water in the desert and streams in the wasteland, to give drink to my people, my chosen, the people I formed for myself that they may proclaim my praise." – Isaiah 43:20, 21

9

MY FATHER DIED TWICE LAST WEEK!
DESERT OF UNFORGIVENESS

Thrival Key: *I Can't, He Can!*

"MY FATHER DIED TWICE LAST WEEK!" MY YOUNG NEIGHBOR EXCLAIMED AFTER he came pounding on our door. At first, I wasn't sure I had heard him correctly. He was speaking in Arabic, and I had only been studying Arabic for a few months. In 2010, my husband and I felt God asked us to make a change, so after twenty years in China, we followed His leading to a country in the Arabian Peninsula.

After hearing our young friend's exclamation, the very next thought I had may seem strange until I explain. I thought, "This boy's father is my least favorite person in the world!" Still, I wanted to understand what he was saying.

I quickly asked an American friend with better language skills to help me. As soon as we could, we went to visit this boy's family, hoping for clarity. We discovered that my young friend had, indeed, said his father died twice.

His meaning was that his father had had two heart attacks. The previous week, his father's heart had stopped two times. We learned the doctors were planning an emergency surgery the following week.

After leaving our Arab neighbor's home, I found myself in deep inner conflict. I knew that I needed to pray for this man, but I didn't know how. How could I pray for this man who had dared to grope me in front of the rest of his family?

I remember that awful incident vividly. Normally, men in Arab Gulf countries do not sit with the ladies. Most houses have separate rooms for men and women to gather in.

This family was very poor, however, and only had one sitting room. The man of the house had come home for lunch, while I was visiting the mother and her daughters.

The ladies served their husband and father, and then the whole family of twelve sat beside him. As their guest, I was served at the same time, along with the head of the house.

During our lunchtime, we had a lively conversation about the prophets. The man of the house colorfully told stories about each prophet. As he spoke about each, he would gesture with his hands. With each new story, he raised yet another finger and pointed to it, as if counting.

When he had finished pointing, and all his fingers were raised. Suddenly and very unexpectedly, he put his hands on my breasts. He did this for what seemed to be about three seconds, then took his hands back and continued to tell his story.

He continued to speak as if his actions were part of his speech! He behaved as if this was a totally normal thing to do! I was absolutely stunned. I was so surprised by this that I remember being in a mental fog.

I thought, "Did this really happen?" I was shocked! It was surreal. I politely said my good-byes and thanked the neighbors for the meal. Then, I quickly crossed the dusty road to return home and tell my husband what had happened.

I avoided my neighbor's husband for several months after that day. In the Arab Gulf, it was a crime for him to have groped me. Had I told the police, they would have imprisoned him immediately. They would have wanted to uphold the honor of their religion.

After discussing the situation with my husband, we decided not to report him. I knew Satan would use a report to halt the wonderful relationships I had with his wife and their children. Instead, my husband and I agreed that I would only visit my friend's home when I was certain her husband was gone.

God gave me the grace to continue visiting my neighbor's home. And, as time went on, we had deeper and deeper conversations about Christ's love for all of us. Even so, my mind labeled the man of that house "my least favorite person."

Now, I was emotionally conflicted because this same man was due to have a surgery which could mean life or death. This knowledge made me uneasy. I knew that I needed to forgive him.

This was something I had chosen to do immediately after his violating offense. I chose to forgive with my mind, but my emotions weren't yet following. I wanted to forgive him because I had learned that holding a grudge only hurts the one who has it.

I also knew Christ told us we must forgive from our hearts if we want to receive forgiveness from Him. **I told God that I wasn't capable of forgiving him. I really did not know how.** I asked the Lord to give me His ability to do what I could not.

The Holy Spirit began to work in me. He replaced my loathing for the man and gave me an attitude of compassion toward him instead. I couldn't sleep at night knowing he might die without ever having heard the only way to God, our Father, is through Jesus Christ.

His faith had taught him that a relationship with God was not possible. He could only hope that he would spend eternity in heaven if he was "good enough." Because of this, I knew if he died, he would spend eternity in hell. I also knew this is never God's perfect will.

God doesn't want anyone to spend eternity in torment separated from Him. I was reminded that Scripture says God has ordained the exact times and places that we live (Psalm 37:23).

I remembered the fact that it was more than a coincidence that we lived in that exact neighborhood. I believed it was for the purpose of sharing Christ's love with all who lived there. This man needed a cure, both physically and spiritually!

Christ has provided a cure for our spiritual cancer. The problem is that God's exclusive cure hasn't yet been globally distributed. He gave His followers the command to go and proclaim His Good News everywhere for this very reason.

What had stirred my husband and me to live in the Arab world in the first place was this knowledge. After the Holy Spirit gave me His love for my violator, I could not rest until I found a way to share about Jesus Christ with him.

This can be a tricky thing to do while living in a one hundred percent Muslim country. Though difficult, I was determined that "my least favorite person" would hear about God's cure, no matter the cost. He needed to know that Jesus Christ professed to be the only way, the only cure for his spiritually sick soul.

I laid awake at night, trying to decide what to do. I found it easy to speak with almost everyone else, but I had been avoiding this man. How could I share the hope that was within me with *him*?

I chose to fast for three days. This is my default every time I need specific wisdom. God has always been faithful to give me answers after a fast. I knew He would continue to be faithful. Scripture promises that God will give us wisdom when we ask for it in faith. I am so thankful that He never lies!

Sure enough, after fasting, I was given a special gift of faith. I marched across the street, empowered with a holy boldness not my own. I told my neighbor's husband I had a message from God for him, my Bible fully visible to any who would have seen me.

At this point in time, he had been greatly humbled. He eagerly listened to me as I shared the story of God healing a woman whose bleeding wouldn't stop. God had prepared his heart to listen. I suppose that facing the prospect of death had this effect.

I told him that Jesus was alive in heaven, sitting with God, the Father. I told him that Jesus still heals today. Then I told him God would heal him if he agreed to let me pray for him in Jesus' name. I was thrilled to hear him agree to such a prayer.

God gave me the gift of faith to trust that his body would be healed. In Jesus' name, I prayed that he would live to learn more of God's love for him. I left him with a copy of an Arabic New Testament, and he received it with great reverence toward God and His Holy Book.

I was overjoyed to learn that the doctor canceled the scheduled surgery. When they examined my friend's husband and his pre-surgery information, they found he no longer had a heart problem!

God is Good! He sends His rain on the righteous and the unrighteous alike. He is worthy of our praise! He gives good gifts to those who will ask.

Praise the Lord! He makes it possible to forgive. **When I knew I couldn't find a way, I was certain that the Lord would help me if I asked!** Thank you, Lord! When I can't do something, I can step into Your yoke and trust that You can by Your power!

THRIVAL KEY - I CAN'T... HE CAN!

"... apart from me you can do nothing." – John 15:5

"I can do all things through Christ who gives me strength." – Philippians 4:13

"YOU USED TO BE SO PATHETIC!" MY OLD MIDDLE-SCHOOL FRIEND SAID AFTER seeing me for the first time in over 20 years. Fate, it would seem, caused us to bump into each other at a mall. We were in a different state than when we had attended school together in Iowa. This, it would seem, was quite the "coincidence."

Hearing her words made me chuckle. I was happy that she saw a difference in me. This friend truly knew what I used to be like before I gave my life to Christ. When we were teenagers, I was terribly insecure. I had absolutely no sense of self-worth or self-confidence. I *had* been pathetic. I was pathetically *trying* to live my life in my own strength and fell flat!

I had believed many lies whispered to my mind. I was convinced I was stupid, ugly, and that I couldn't do anything right. Some people need to be convinced that nothing good lives in them. This was not the case with me. I knew it was true. I just didn't know what to do about it.

After I understood that Christ came to do for us what we could not do for ourselves, all that changed. I discovered that He gives the ability to have success in life. He'll do this for anyone willing to ask for His help and let Him lead.

When we choose to **let Christ live through us**, we can have abundant life. I now had a completely different mode of operation. My old friend was quick to ask me what had made the difference.

I was able to share with her that it was God's promise in Scripture that gave me confidence. I wasn't relying on *my* strength anymore but His! I had learned to rely on the Holy Spirit every time I felt inadequate.

Through every season of life, no matter what I have had to face, this principle has been vital for me! **When I had no ability to forgive the man who had accosted me, I could trust that God would give me His ability.** Knowing it was His desire for me to forgive, I told God, "I can't, but I know You can!" I knew He would have to work in me what I simply had no power to do myself.

The movie about Nazi death camps called *The Hiding Place* greatly affected me as a young believer. The Ten Boom family suffered greatly in the camps because of trying to help the Jews. Corrie Ten Boom hated the soldiers that mistreated them and killed her family members. When she asked God to take the hate from her, He did.

Corrie is famous for saying, "When we are powerless to do a thing, it is a great joy that we can come and step inside the ability of Jesus." I learned from Corrie that nothing is impossible for God. If He helped her to forgive, He would do the same for me.

Learning that I could let the ability of Jesus work through me turned my life upside down! I began surrendering to the Holy Spirit's control with every kind of struggle I had.

Some hardships involve our minds, so our thinking needs to be changed. Others come through the limitations of our bodies. At times, our emotions put us in deserts. Whatever the cause, I have found freedom by stepping into Christ's ability.

When depleting, emotional struggles surface, I've learned to offer myself to the Lord, intentionally emptying myself once again. I ask Him to fill me with his power and replace my harmful feelings with His perfect emotions.

When temptations seemed impossible to overcome, I've asked God to give me His strength to overcome them. My confidence is in the Lord's ability now, not mine. It's the secret to living a life that embodies Christ.

That said, I'm continually learning how to stay there without distraction. This vital key sometimes seems like a completely foreign idea, but Scripture speaks much about it. It is actually possible.

Our work overseas has required my husband and me to take psychological tests through the years. Sending organizations want to make sure their people are equipped to deal with stress in a healthy way.

One such test showed my personal confidence level was at 99%. Being a leader who is used to reading test scores, I knew this finding would raise a red flag. It certainly would if I were reviewing someone else's results. It could indicate that I was overly confident in my abilities or was, perhaps, unteachable.

When the counselor asked what I thought about this outcome, I explained my confidence is in Christ's ability... not my own. I told him that if I had taken that test before Jesus was my Lord, my level would have been a flatline 0%!

I went on to explain that it was only because Jesus Christ now lives in me! It is His power I rely on! He has proven himself trustworthy time and time again! Praise God! The counselor was a man who understood this Scriptural principle and had no further questions.

God doesn't want us to live with a "loser" mentality. He doesn't want us walking around feeling hopeless. But he also doesn't want us to have an "I've got this!" mentality.

God doesn't want us to think we are capable of doing anything by ourselves. He wants us to be utterly dependent upon Him. With Jesus, co-dependence is a good thing!

God desires for us to be humbly aware that our every breath is a gift from Him. He wants us to walk victoriously, but to do so with His strength. He wants us to have an "I'm more than a conqueror because of Christ" attitude!

Oh, what freedom comes when there's no pressure to be good in and of ourselves! How wonderful to know that nothing good dwells in me, of my old nature!

What confidence we can have knowing the God of the universe fully backs us up! When we're fully dependent on Him, He blesses us indescribably with His enabling power.

We don't have to work at attaining godliness. Instead, Christ gives us freedom and grace to grow in His likeness. He causes our spirits to soar. When we choose to let Him "take the reins," nothing will be impossible for us!

When I lose my peace or feel discouraged, I recognize that I'm trying to live in my own ability again. I know I've somehow taken my focus off Christ. I'm certain of this because I'm never discouraged when I'm relying on Him.

Satan desperately wants to prevent us from walking in an "I'm more than a conqueror through Christ" mentality. He likes to whisper, "*You can't do it*." He often resorts to telling us the truth about ourselves, hoping we will be self-focused again.

He attacks our minds to distract and hinder us, to stop our gaze on Christ. Our enemy wants us to fail, and not glorify God. Satan is happy to tell us the truth about how miserable we are when left to ourselves.

I've discovered the best remedy for this is to agree with him. I say, "You're right, Satan. I can't, but Christ in me *can*, and He *will*! I'm not relying on *me* anymore! I have surrendered my life to God."

Dispelling the darkness like this, we can move forward in life with complete confidence that God is backing us up. When we agree with the devil about how utterly worthless we are without Christ, it cuts the ground right out from underneath his diabolical attempt to discourage us.

I'm greatly comforted in knowing that God doesn't look for the most highly qualified person to do something. He doesn't operate according to the systems of this world! Hallelujah!

He doesn't look on the outward appearance. God simply looks for hearts that yield to His total control. He looks for those who give Him all the credit and glory. With this in place, He does extraordinary things through ordinary people.

Anything good accomplished in or through my life has only been through intentional, daily surrender to Christ. He chooses the "foolish things of the world to confound the wise." I'm so grateful!

During some of my deepest trials, there have been times I've felt I couldn't survive. My circumstances were beyond my control, and my emotions were swirling about me.

It was in these times that I learned to hold on to the promise of 1 Corinthians 1:8. "He will keep you strong to the very end and blameless on the day of our Lord Christ." We just have to allow Him to be in charge.

When I feel I'm in one of life's deserts, or feel one coming on, I've learned to make a proclamation. I need to hear myself say, "God, I'm taking my hands off the wheel. Please do for me the things I can't deal with on my own at this moment."

It's like being in a car in front of a stop sign when, suddenly, a tornado-like wind hits the car I'm driving. Debris is swirling all around me and it's a scary place to be. I start to feel overwhelmed.

Then, just as this happens, and in answer to my prayer, Jesus knocks on the car door of the driver's side. He motions for me to slide over.

When He gets in, the storm is still swirling, but now I'm not the one who has to navigate how to get through the storm. Everything is calm inside with Jesus in charge, with His hand on the wheel.

This life of embodying Christ is quite opposite to humanism. Humanism indoctrinates us with the lie that nothing is impossible for us if we don't quit. Who hasn't been inspired by the story of *The Little Engine that Could*?

I've learned this is only partially true. Because we are created in God's image, we've been given amazing abilities. And God certainly encourages us to be resilient and teaches persistence.

But true success is much greater than what is defined by society. **True success glorifies God. This only comes through reliance on Him, not our own determination or strength.** All earthly accomplishments will be burnt up, having no eternal value unless done for the Lord.

My confidence in belonging to God is that He has the final word on any situation I'm in. As I obey Him, He orders my steps and works in and through me to bring light to the darkness, to bring hope to the hopeless.

He empowers me to be His ambassador on earth. With His Spirit living in us, we can do everything He directs us to do. All of heaven's resources are available to us when we surrender to His Spirit.

1 Corinthians says, "Such confidence as this is ours through Christ before God. Not that we are competent in ourselves to claim anything for ourselves, but our competence comes from God. He has made us competent ministers of a new covenant."

It also says, "Therefore, since we have such a hope, we are very bold." God gives us a holy boldness when we side with Him against our old natures. We have His boldness when we empty ourselves to allow Him to live in and through us.

He never fails us. God, our wonderful Father in heaven, is delighted to have children who trust Him so fully. He is always there to catch us if we start to fall. Even as I write this, the old Jesus movement song "Jesus Never Fails" runs through my head! Hallelujah, this is truth!

Time and time again, Christ's faithfulness has been proven to me. When I didn't know what to do or how to do it, I would say, "God, live through me. I'm stepping into your yoke now."

Sharon, one of my spiritual mentors likes to quote, "If God brings you to it, He'll bring you through it!" I have an absolute confidence this is true.

I only fail if *I* keep trying to do His will, instead of embracing my weakness and accepting God's strength to do it. We succeed when we trust Him to empower and work in us.

The Creator of the universe strongly supports those whose heart is fully given to Him. We cannot go wrong! Thank you, God, for making it possible to live through Christ!

QUESTIONS TO PONDER: CAN YOU SAY, "I NO LONGER LIVE, BUT CHRIST Jesus lives in me," as the apostle Paul said? If not, what is preventing you from saying this?

PRAYER: THANK YOU, LORD, THAT YOU WANT US TO SUCCEED IN LIFE with You! Thank You, Lord, that You make it possible. Please forgive me for attempting to do anything in the power of my old self. I want to let my human nature die daily, and I choose to side with You against it. Please empower me to do Your will. Help me to surrender areas of my life that aren't yet given over to You. I trust You to help me do that. As You help me, I'll say "yes" to You. In Jesus Christ's name, Amen.

10

THEY DIED ANYWAY

DESERT OF GRIEF

Thrival Key: *When I Can't Understand, God's Still Good*

Though he slay me, yet will I hope in him. – Job 13:15

"HE HUNG HIMSELF!" WHAT SHOCKING WORDS I HEARD MY BROTHER stammering to say on the other end of the phone call. It took a few seconds for me to wrap my mind around what I'd just heard.

He said that an ambulance had been called, and they were trying to revive his youngest, 16-year-old son while we spoke. This news was like having the wind knocked out of me, and I didn't know what to say or do. But my default is to take things to God in times of need.

I immediately told my brother that I was going to hang up and pray. I couldn't find the words, so I chose to let the Holy Spirit pray through me instead, using the heavenly language that God gave me when I first surrendered my life to His control.

I was deep in intercession when, just a few minutes later my brother called back and said, "He's gone. My baby is gone." I couldn't believe what I was hearing. I don't remember what I said to my brother, but after I hung up the phone, I continued to be in a state of shock for most of the day.

As soon as possible, family members from across the U.S. converged on a small town in California for the memorial service of our loved one. The invaluable comfort of a loving family in such times of tragedy is hard to put into words.

We didn't know what to say, but we were together. Everyone pitched in to organize food supplies that my brother and sister-in-law's church so lovingly sent us every day. We sat around, trying to cheer each other up with positive memories, and we assisted with chores needing to be done. With these things, we kept ourselves occupied.

On the day of the memorial service, I was utterly amazed at the amount of grace and supernatural peace surrounding my brother and his wife. They shared with amazing calmness about the blessing the life of their son had been to them. The church was completely full.

Caring for the emotional needs of the crowd, they gave away countless reassuring hugs to distraught teenagers and friends. I knew that many, many people were lifting them up in prayer while God's grace carried them supernaturally that day.

Two years prior to this dreadful event, my husband and I had flown back home to the U.S. for a visit. Arriving in the Midwest, we were excited to see our family and hug them once again.

Our oldest son lived in Texas, so, unfortunately, we were forced to wait a few weeks before our work schedule allowed us to travel so far south to see him. However, our middle son and his family, as well as our youngest son, lived in a neighboring state.

We hadn't seen our children for a year, and we could hardly wait to do so. But we had some appointments and speaking engagements to attend to first, along the way.

We shared our stories from overseas with a Wednesday evening church group, and then we planned to drive through the night to see our kids as soon as possible. Our daughter-in-law was pregnant, and we had received texts telling us that she was in labor!

We were amazed at God's timing, allowing us to be in the U.S. during this momentous time. It was hard to concentrate fully on the message I was sharing that night because I couldn't stop thinking about the arrival of our new grandchild.

My phone rang while I was speaking. Forgetting to turn off my ringer, I apologized to the listening crowd. Yet, as soon as I finished, I excitedly checked to see if the baby had been born.

Instead of good news, I had an urgent message from my son asking for prayer because their baby had been born but wasn't able to breathe. The paramedics were still working on him at the time.

I immediately shared this news with the crowd, asking for prayers, and I went to the altar to ask God to intervene. I wept and prayed intensely.

I recalled that Jesus said if we had faith as small as a mustard seed, we could speak to mountains to be moved.

I also remembered the story of Jesus raising Lazarus from the dead. I knew that nothing was too difficult for Him. With as much faith as I had within me, I asked God to do a miracle.

After praying, I called our son, only to discover that our new grandchild was now in heaven with Jesus. I was in disbelief as we drove through the night to be with our grieving children.

Though I knew our new grandson had died, I remembered all the past times God had given miraculous answers through prayer. I remembered the principle Jesus taught, that we often don't have things because we don't ask God for them. So, with an urgent, last resort effort, and trying to have the faith of a little child, I dared to ask Him to "raise the dead."

I fully trusted God with my request, but the horrendous truth sunk in, after we received another phone call. **Our kids were now having to make funeral plans instead of having a celebration.**

Even though our daughter-in-law had had a perfect pregnancy and delivery, their dear Everton was found to have a rare gene mutation that negatively affected the part of his DNA allowing him to breathe outside the womb. Both my husband and I were stunned.

Three years before the tragic death of our just new grandson, my best friend's husband had to be committed to an Alzheimer's care facility. He had slowly been declining, while my friend desperately attempted to care for her husband at home.

One night, not knowing who his wife was, my best friend's husband tried to strangle her, being afraid for his life. She was in the middle of trying to change an adult diaper when her husband took the bedsheet and wrapped it around her neck.

He had been a pastor, and we had helped pioneer a new church with him and his wife. My husband was the worship leader, and I helped with the youth group.

We believe the Bible teaches that healing is provided for us through the work Jesus did on the cross (Isaiah 53:5). He always does more than enough. He provided for our sin *and* our sicknesses. We have prayed for lots of sick people and have seen many of them physically healed.

Yet, when we prayed for our pastor friend, everything we knew to do didn't seem to be adequate. We haven't yet seen His physical healing, and he has been in an Alzheimer's care facility for over six years now.

Today, I still believe that Jesus came to destroy the works of the devil. I still believe He commands his followers to pray for the sick and to preach that God's Kingdom is near. I still believe that He gives His followers His authority to bring healing in His name.

That said, I simply don't understand why we don't see answers to our prayers sometimes, not in the way we expect, anyway. But because God is God, I must believe there are circumstances existing that we mere mortals could never understand.

I am sure that most everyone reading this has had times when they haven't understood why our good God has allowed something tragic to happen.

We can't understand many things regarding God's dealings with us... what He does or does not do. Why God allows desert seasons of grief, full of tragedy or disaster, often remains a mystery.

In these recent years, after experiencing the death of our new grandson and nephew, along with our friend's Alzheimer's, I've experienced many waves of grief. Adding to my sadness, my Dad passed away a few months ago after complications due to COVID 19. The deep sense of loss has been difficult to describe.

With all the grief that we humans suffer, some have told me they have a hard time believing God exists. They don't understand how God could be good while allowing us to experience so much pain. This has caused me to reexamine my faith and what I believe.

It is common, when in a desert of grief, to question many things about our faith in God. I've learned that's okay with Him. He understands grief and cares about our feelings. He wants us to know what we believe and why we believe it.

"Grief, like love, is unique," my brother said at a church service while remembering his son's suicide. I have found this to be absolutely true.

So, too, are the methods used to help people move forward in their grief. What works for one, may not work for another. That said, here are some tools my dear ones have used:

One practical method my brother implemented was to write a poem and post it on Facebook. His poem expressed all the questions in his heart and reaffirmed his love for his son. It also expressed his desire to keep others from experiencing the same tragedy.

My sister-in-law found comfort by relying on memorizing Scriptures. Psalm 25:4-5 was especially significant, and she daily remembered these words, "Show me your ways, O Lord, teach me your paths; guide me in your truth and teach me, for you are God my Savior, and my hope is in you all day long."

Creating a video expressing their heartfelt sorrows and questions was another healthy coping mechanism that our good friends from India used. It helped them move forward after their daughter's suicide.

Carla, our daughter-in-law, says she received comfort from others. Though they hadn't experienced what she had, she said, "Just having people acknowledge my grief and that it was hard and was something they would never understand was helpful."

She also says that Romans 8:28 was strong in her heart from the beginning. She focused on the truth that God was working ALL things together for the good of those who love Him. She told herself, "He will not cause suffering without bringing something new."

Some of the most helpful words she received from others were, "Take it one breath at a time, one step at a time... to get through the hardest parts." They told her she would know joy again.

At the beginning of his grief, our son, Wesley, didn't want to talk to a single person. He couldn't even be in a room with someone comfortably unless they had been through what he'd experienced. He then chose to process the same tragedy as his wife in yet another unique way. He made a conscious choice to not be angry at God. Though he was devastated by their loss, he told himself, "I'm not going to go down that road. I'm not going to go down that angry, questioning path."

The thrival key that I have personally relied on throughout my life *when I've been numb with pain and can't understand, is to remind myself that God's still good. His character hasn't changed just because my circumstances have.* In my bewilderment, I've had to lean on this truth continuously in the past few years…

This chapter doesn't seem to have the miracle solutions or "happy ending" that the stories in the previous chapters had…or does it?

When I can't understand, God's still good.

THRIVAL KEY – WHEN I CAN'T UNDERSTAND, GOD'S STILL GOOD

"FOR THE LORD IS GOOD AND HIS LOVE ENDURES FOREVER; HIS **faithfulness continues through all generations" – Psalm 100:5**

Daily, as I watch the evening news, I am confronted with the fact that our world is full of pain, suffering, and evil. It makes me sad. I am even more grieved knowing that many people think Christians, or Christ-followers, accept all these terrible things as God's perfect will.

Because of this, multitudes have turned their backs on Christianity. Many scoff at the idea that our world was created by intelligent design. They can't accept that a good being exists who has supreme power and cares about the happenings on earth. **They can't understand how a good God could allow such suffering.**

There are many scholarly, theological answers given in response. Among these are summarized answers like this one: God blessed all

He created and called it good. In the beginning, pain, suffering, and evil didn't exist. It has never been what He wanted. However, *he desired for humans to have a free will*, so He gave them a choice. Would they obey Him or decide that they knew what was better than He did?

The Bible says Adam and Eve, the first man and woman, decided to disobey God. They were lured into doing evil in God's sight when the fallen angel, Satan, encouraged it. This brought sin into the world. *Sin is the cause of all the grief that has existed since that time.*

The continuing, scriptural argument goes on to say that God knew these things would happen from before time but made a way for us even when we didn't deserve His mercy. Because God is good and loves all the people in the world, He doesn't want anyone to suffer permanent, spiritual death. So, He sent the exact representation of His being to earth in the form of a man. Jesus Christ, God's Son, God Himself, came to earth for the expressed purpose of destroying the works of the devil, who is the god of this present world.

However, humankind doesn't have to be estranged from God any longer because of our sin. Christ made forgiveness possible. He will protect and defend all those who choose to call themselves by His name. He said that He would work *all things* together for the good of those who love Him (Romans 8:28). God will even use the worst desert seasons and pain that come our way and spin them into something good for His children.

Jesus warned us that we would have many troubles in this world. But He also encouraged us by saying He has overcome it (John 16:33).

Because He's good, He's not going to allow this present world and the evil in it to exist forever. Jesus Christ will return to earth someday and will banish all that causes pain and suffering. He will rule and reign on the earth. In the end, God is going to create a new heaven and a new earth. There will be no more sorrow and tears. **He's planning on making all things new!**

But only those who have chosen to trust in God and His ways will live with Him forever.

Because God is good, He is also just. He must allow the present situation to continue on earth to give all humans a choice. He's willing to wait before putting His future, irreversible actions in place. He patiently waits to give each person an opportunity to choose eternal life with Him, through Christ Jesus.

This reads a lot like some of the superhero movies that have recently been released in the theaters, doesn't it? It sounds like a fairy tale made up by someone with a very vivid imagination. I agree. The Bible tells *an amazing story*. And it is a story that I choose to believe as the truth!

After much contemplation and logical reasoning, this story makes sense to me. I believe that, in the end, God is making all things new. This satisfies my mind when I'm in a desert season of grief. I know that the loss I have will be resolved in the light of a future eternity with God in heaven…at least I can make some sense of what has happened.

Christ Jesus said that His kingdom was not of *this* world (John 18:36). I can appreciate the fact that God is allowing this present, trouble-filled world to continue because He is patiently waiting for more people to choose Him. He is like a farmer who greatly desires to harvest his crops but is willing to wait for the perfect timing and conditions to have the best results.

This world is just temporary, but it allows humans an opportunity to willingly choose God as the ultimate authority over their lives. After all, heaven will only be filled with people who want Him to be in control!

That said, these Biblical truths are all well and good for how everything will turn out in the end, but they don't necessarily help me, emotionally, in the here and now. When our new grandson didn't live for more than a few minutes, I was stunned at first, then full of sorrow. When my sweet nephew hung himself, it caused me to question God. "Why, Lord?" "How could you allow this to happen?" I was disheartened.

Our friend has had severe Alzheimer's for so long, I am bewildered. To comfort me emotionally, theology and Biblical answers about the future aren't what I need. I need more than facts. *I need emotional encouragement and healing.*

I have found when I am in profound sadness and can't understand why God has allowed a loss of some kind, I must remember just one thing to lift my spirits. I must remember that God's still good.

When I trust the knowledge that God's still good, despite the tragedies, it encourages me in a multitude of ways. **Because God is good:**

- **I can trust Him.** He always does what is right. He's just and true in all His ways. *This makes me feel secure.*
- **I can believe Him because He never lies.** I can know with certainty that *I have hope* for a future day in heaven. My sorrow won't last forever. I don't have to grieve in the same way as those who have no hope.
- **He is faithful.** He always takes care of His children, doing what is always ultimately best for them. I know that He sees factors in my circumstances that I can't begin to

comprehend. *I feel cared for* when I recall all the times in my life that He's proved Himself real to me… I don't have to keep it all together, emotionally. I can rest in His care, crying on His shoulders.

- **He gives me good things.** When I remember the many good things that I still have, it makes me thankful. *Being thankful makes me smile.*

- **God loves me.** Because He loves us, He turns our worst situations and their pain into something good for us. And then He will use us to help others in need with the same comfort we've received from Him. *This reminds me that I still have a purpose and makes me feel significant. It helps me move forward.*

God's still good even when my prayers seem unanswered, or if He answers by saying, "No." I believe this with all my heart. He's proven Himself to me in such a real way that I could never deny Jesus Christ as my Lord and Savior. I know Him as my best friend and the lover of my soul.

I've come to understand that in God's goodness, He uses my desert seasons like soap to wash away any self-dependence I may have. He may not have caused the deserts, but He's more clearly seen at work in me when I allow Him to carry me during them. When I am weak and He's carrying me, then I am made strong. This brings Jesus much more glory than anything I could ever hope to bring Him with my own efforts.

I've learned to find value in my deserts and embrace them. I'm learning to lean into God more through the pain and hardships. I'm learning not to waste them, but to see them as an opportunity to tell the world how very good God is. I choose to see them as opportunities for Jesus Christ to shine through me. People will listen to someone they can identify with.

My mother-in-law, twice a widow says it best. She lost her first husband to an electrical accident and another to cancer. She has said, "We, the black and blued with suffering, understand by experience. When we were together as a couple, we had a strong faith. *After the deaths of my two husbands, that faith didn't change because God doesn't change.* Though my union with my husbands is no longer, my husbands' deaths don't change my union with God. God wastes nothing. He will use the pain we've gone through to help someone else." God's still good.

So, it seems, my desert stories of grief have a happy ending after all! *Because I am His child, I can't lose!* **When I don't understand, God's still good!**

QUESTIONS TO PONDER: HOW CAN YOU SEE THAT GOD WAS GOOD TO YOU IN your past deserts of grief? What have you read in this chapter that you want to remember to help you in the future?

PRAYER: LORD, MY GOD, I CONFESS THAT I DON'T UNDERSTAND SOME OF the things You've allowed in my life. But today, I choose to trust that You are still good, despite them. As it says in 2 Corinthians 4:18, I choose not to fix my eyes on what is seen. I choose not to focus on my deserts or my grief. Instead, I choose to focus on the unseen…on You and on the fact that I always have hope. I know that what is seen is temporary, but You are eternal. Your love for me will never end. Thank You for all the good things You've given me. Thank You for being good. In Jesus' name, Amen.

CONCLUSION

Genuine miracles are a common occurrence, but I often don't recognize them as such. For instance, there are times when I'm running late for an appointment due to traffic issues. I may be frustrated, but God is directing my steps for a purpose I can't understand.

I've heard stories of people missing their flights only to discover that they would have been on the plane that crashed. Perhaps I should be praising God that my flights were canceled?

I've learned inconvenient times in my life can turn out to be divinely ordained. Like when an item at the check-out counter wasn't being read by the computer correctly. This forced a grocery worker to check on the price. It was seemingly a long wait in his absence, but it allowed me the time to have an encouraging conversation with another person in line who needed it.

I've had a stranger show up and ask if he or she can help me. They just happen to have the information necessary for me, at the precise moment I needed it.

At other times, I've had people mention, in passing, the exact words I needed to encourage and lift my spirits. Or I just happen to find the answer to something I've been searching for while skimming a magazine.

It's amazing how many "coincidences" happen to us when we've committed our lives to serve the living God. And those "coincidences," or unrecognized miracles, seem to multiply when we've committed our concerns to Him in prayer. God answers prayer.

Praise God! He still does sensational and undeniable miracles today. He still does things that make people stand in awe while His mighty power is on display. But I also praise and thank Him for times when I don't see the extraordinary or astounding.

"Why haven't I seen one of those awesome miracles?" some may ask. My answer is simple: I don't know. I don't know why I have been spared two times from a major medical incident because of a miraculous healing, and why, at another time, my non-functioning shoulder required surgery.

I don't pretend to know. However, one thing I DO know is that God always does what is right, and I trust Him. I believe His Word is true, *much truer* than what my present circumstances seem to dictate.

I will continue to have faith in God's promises. I will continue to ask Him for spectacular, needed miracles and trust Him while expecting them. I encourage you to ask the Lord for them too! He has not stopped doing miracles.

The most important thing is for our focus to be on the Lord. It's not the miracles that I seek, but the One who gives them. When we seek His glory, and ask for a miracle for His name's sake, we can be assured that our motives are pure.

So, even though I'm expecting a miracle but don't receive one, when I don't know "Why?," I'm ok with that.

My default is to go with what I do know... and that is always the fact that **I'm in really good hands.** My God, who gave His best for me, continues to love me and is working on my behalf... even when it doesn't feel like it.

Especially when I don't feel like it, I trust this is true!

All of life is a miracle. Each system of creation is a miracle. All of nature displays the glory of God! He sends rain on the righteous and the unrighteous alike.

The Creator of our universe is GOOD. He is the only One that is worthy of all our attention, all our love, all our devotion, all of our lives, and all of our praise.

It has been my hope that by reading some of these stories and "Thrival Keys," your focus and attention are more upwardly directed, pointing you nearer to God in your relationship with Him than before.

If you have been discouraged, I trust you've had glimmers of hope rise in your heart. I've prayed that you'll be stirred in your faith to trust God for more, focusing your eyes on Him to see possibilities of better days ahead.

If all God's miracles could be recorded from the creation of the world till now, it would astound us. **Yet, the *greatest miracle of all* for any**

person willing to believe and receive it, is having a new life... a new beginning made possible with God.

A spiritual rebirth happens when we choose to follow Jesus Christ as Lord and the One that we let control our lives. We ask Him to forgive our past sins and invite God's Holy Spirit to dwell in us. Allowing Him to guide and direct us for the rest of our lives, we begin a personal relationship with God that brings freedom and inner peace.

If I could choose just one of the stories in this book for you to remember, it would be the one recording the miracle of my new life in Christ. I love Him with all my heart and will forever sing His praise! He's rescued me from myself! Praise His Name... He alone is worthy of all I am and have.

"May the God of hope fill you with all joy and peace as you trust in Him, so that you may overflow with hope by the power of the Holy Spirit." – Romans 15:13

PRAYER SUGGESTIONS

I suggest the following prayers for anyone desiring to surrender more fully to God.

For those who are convinced that Jesus Christ is God's truth and the only way to eternal life:

God in heaven, our Creator, I humbly come to You because I believe that Jesus Christ is Your chosen way for me to have my sin and shame erased before You. I ask that You please accept me as your son/daughter and forgive me my sins and take away my shame from before You. I invite your Holy Spirit to dwell in me and teach me and empower me to live for You. I choose to give control of my life to You from this day forward. I ask this of You, Holy God in heaven, in the name of Jesus Christ because of the provision You've made for me through him. I want to have a new birth of Your Holy Spirit. Thank You for accepting me and making me into a new creation. I want to live to praise Your name. Amen.

For those who are still seeking God's truth about Jesus Christ:

Almighty God, most Merciful and Compassionate, our Creator who cares for us all, I believe that You exist and always see what is happening in my life. I believe that You are the Rewarder of those who diligently seek You. I want to seek You and do what pleases You. Please help me understand more about having eternal life in heaven. I want to know I will live eternally there. If Jesus Christ is Your only chosen way for me to be forgiven, I ask that You please reveal this to me. Show me Your Truth. When Jesus Christ was on earth, it is recorded that He said, "I am The Way, The Truth, and The Life. No one comes to God, the Father, except by me." Almighty God, I want You to be my Lord, and I ask You to guide me and reveal Your truth to me about Jesus Christ. I choose to live for You and obey You. I want to obey Your plan. I need Your guidance. Amen.

A brief word for my Muslim friends:

It is written in the *Injeel* that God calls Jesus Christ "His Son." This is NOT because He had a normal, human origin, but because He was sent from God, His heavenly "Father." He is unlike any other person who has ever walked on the face of this earth.

His mother was human, yet, literally became pregnant when the power of Almighty God came upon her. Jesus Christ is unlike any other prophet regarding His miraculous life's beginning.

Regarding His recorded miracles and His miraculous, bodily resurrection from death, there's never been anyone like Christ Jesus. Over 500 witnesses saw Him alive after his death.

No other prophet was sinless. This is what made it possible for Jesus to be the substitute sacrifice to make payment for the sins of humanity in a just way. He came to earth for the purpose of giving his life. No one else in recorded history has provided for all our shame to be erased.

God provided this "lamb" for us as a substitute, just as He did for Abraham. He no longer was required to offer his son as a sacrifice.

It is written that Almighty God requires a sacrifice of blood to cover our sins. The blood of animals is only temporary, but the blood that Jesus offered will cover our sins once and for all if we allow Him to. We can receive God's provision for us through Christ, so we don't have to spend eternity in hell, paying the price ourselves.

Jesus Christ came to earth to give us this choice of spiritual rebirth: the choice of eternal life with God in heaven. This offer is given to anyone who is willing to go to Him.

In Loving Memory of My Dad

"Pebbles, Stones and <u>The Rock</u>"

Day by day as we walk through this life,
In a world full of sin – full of strife;
We step on pebbles, we step on stones.
We have problems in our work and our homes.
The paths we've tried are not always smooth,
There are pebbles to clear and stones to move;
People taunt us and question our stand.
They spread disbelief throughout this land.
When we feel that no one shares our load,
We should pray and look on down the road;
We need to call upon the One who'll care,
Who gave us his Son – His love to share.
The Rock on which I will take my stand,
Is the foundation God gives to man.
The Son of God to die for our sins,
So the battle of life we may now win.

Clifton C. Schmitt
November 17, 1985